THE
WILTSHIRE
REGIMENT
1914-1959

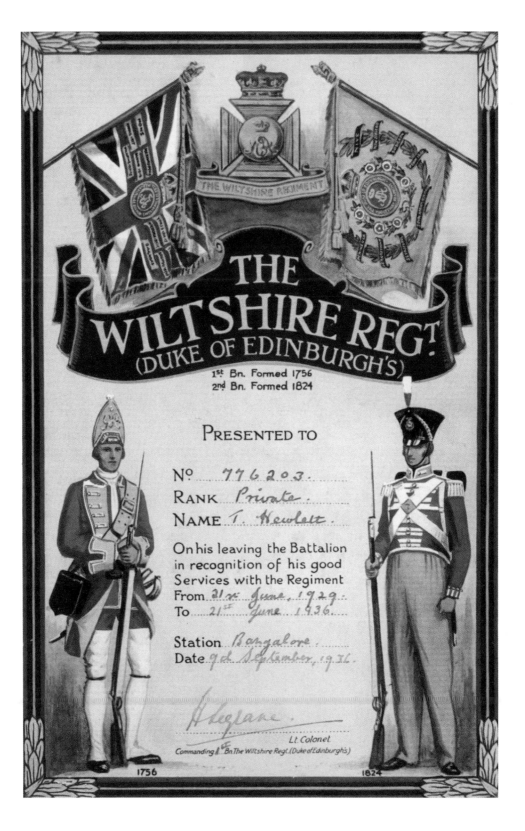

THE
WILTSHIRE
REGIMENT

1914-1959

MARTIN McINTYRE

TEMPUS

Frontispiece: Shortly after the First World War, the Wiltshire Regiment started a tradition of presenting a commemorative discharge certificate to soldiers upon completion of their service with the regiment. With a break during the Second World War, the practice continued up to 1959, when the Wiltshires amalgamated with the Royal Berkshire Regiment. This certificate belonged to Pte T. Hewlett, who joined the regiment in 1929 and was discharged in Bangalore, India, in 1936, having served seven years with the Colours. After leaving the regiment, he would have served for a further five years on the reserve.

First published 2006
Reprinted 2007

Tempus Publishing Limited
The Mill, Brimscombe Port,
Stroud, Gloucestershire, GL5 2QG
www.tempus-publishing.com

British Library Cataloguing in Publication Data.
A catalogue record for this book is available from the British Library.

ISBN 978 0 7524 3757 6

Typesetting and origination by Tempus Publishing Limited.
Printed in Great Britain.

Contents

Left: The Wiltshire Regiment, around 1914, as depicted by the illustrator Harry Payne. Here he shows a Regimental sergeant major and a private soldier of the regiment wearing the familiar scarlet jackets. This uniform was reserved for ceremonial occasions – khaki had been worn on a day-to-day basis for some years by all line infantry regiments. The 1st Battalion wore this dress only weeks before the outbreak of the First World War.

Below: 1st Battalion, Tidworth, *c.*1914. Led by the commanding officer and Corps of Drums, the battalion march back to Jellalabad Barracks after a ceremonial parade, probably the last before the start of the First World War. When the mobilisation order was received, the scarlet jackets would have been returned to the quartermaster's stores.

Introduction and Acknowledgements

The Wiltshire Regiment (Duke of Edinburgh's) existed as a unit in the British Army Order of Battle from 1756–1959, when it was amalgamated with the Royal Berkshire Regiment (Princess Charlotte of Wales') to form the Duke of Edinburgh's Royal Regiment (Berkshire & Wiltshire). The 62nd of Foot, later the 1st Battalion Wiltshire Regiment, was raised in Torbay in 1756, while the 99th of Foot, later the 2nd Battalion Wiltshire Regiment, was formed in Glasgow in 1824.

This volume opens with the regiment's entry into the First World War; like all regiments at that time, the front-line battalions increased substantially in numbers. In total, the county of Wiltshire raised thirteen battalions during the war. Most fought on the Western Front, but the 1st/4th served in India, Egypt and Palestine, the 2nd/4th in India, the 5th Battalion in Gallipoli and Mesopotamia, and the 7th Battalion in Salonika.

After the First World War the regiment reverted to two regular battalions rotating on foreign service, with one territorial battalion serving in Wiltshire. Between the world wars, the regiment served in Ireland, Hong Kong, India and Shanghai on active service, and had tours of duty in Egypt and Palestine.

On the outbreak of the Second World War, the regiment again swelled its ranks to meet the challenge, serving in France, Italy, Burma, India and Germany. The 4th Territorial Battalion expanded, forming the 5th Battalion, with both fighting side-by-side in the 43rd Wessex Division. At the end of the war, the 1st Battalion remained in India assisting the civil authorities during the partition, after which they returned to England. In 1948, both the 1st and 2nd Regular Battalions amalgamated in Krefeld, Germany, as part of the post-war Army reductions. The 1st Battalion then served in Germany, Hong Kong and England; they then returned to active service in Cyprus where they served for three gruelling years during the EOKA campaign. During this campaign they earned the distinction of being the longest serving Infantry regiment on the island.

After the Second World War, the territorial battalions were disbanded, with the 4th Battalion being reformed in 1947, serving until 1967 when they became part of the Wessex Regiment (TA). The regimental cap badge worn throughout the period covered by this book was the Cross pattée, adopted by the 62nd of Foot when serving in the Mediterranean in 1806, and the Coronet and Cypher of the Duke of Edinburgh, which was authorised as the crest of the 99th in 1874. The only change made to the cap badge was when the present Duke of Edinburgh became the Colonel-in-Chief in 1954, and his personal cipher replaced the older one.

As with all regiments, they acquired nicknames over the years. The 62nd (1st Battalion) were known as 'The Springers', which was earned for their alertness and rapidity of movement in action during the American War of Independence in 1777 while employed as light infantry; the 99th (2nd Battalion) were known as 'The Queens Pets' due to their always being chosen to find the guard on the Royal Pavilion in Aldershot during 1857. The sartorial elegance of the 99th, with their ostentatious adornment of gold lace, is believed to have done much to popularise the expression 'dressed up to the nines'.

All Wiltshire battalions were known as 'The Moonrakers', after the legend that some Wiltshire men who indulged in smuggling, were surprised by Excise officials while in the process of removing hidden kegs of brandy from a pond. The story goes that the smugglers excused their behaviour by stating that they were trying to rake out a fine cheese that had been dropped into the water. As it was a bright, moonlit night, the Excise officials thought that the 'simple country folk' had mistaken the reflection of the moon on the water as something more tangible, and left them to their pursuits. Several Wiltshire villages and towns lay claim to the pond in question, but Devizes is considered to be the favourite, which is the home town of the Regimental Depot Le Marchant Barracks.

The style and presentation of this book has been dictated by the quantity and quality of images available. The photographs have been selected to give as wide a coverage as possible of the regiment's activities, both in war and peace. It is, however, restricted at times by the availability of photographs, particularly during active service. Every effort has been made to achieve equality in the cover given to different battalions of the regiment; this has not been an easy task as, despite the many hundreds of photographs to choose from, some battalions kept comprehensive photographic albums, while the compendiums of others have not survived the passage of time. The apparent over-representation of the 1st Battalion during the First World War, and the 4th and 5th Battalions during the Second World War, is due solely to the prevalence of images from this time – a luxury that was not afforded to all battalions. Some of them have appeared in the Regimental Journal, but the majority have never been previously reproduced and, for conservation reasons, are held in the Regimental archives, unavailable for viewing by the general public.

The captions are subsidiary and are intended to place the pictures in context, providing details of circumstances, dates and, where known, individual identities. Every effort has been made to portray as many regimental heroes and characters as possible, but it has only been practical to give the briefest resumes of their careers.

I hope this book conveys throughout a sense of the family spirit of the Wiltshire Regiment, both in terms of brothers-in-arms, drawn mainly from the County of Wiltshire, and also to the continuity of families serving in the regiment, generation after generation. It is this spirit that has been such a great source of tenacity during battles of the past. Furthermore, it continued after the amalgamation into the Duke of Edinburgh's Royal Regiment, and today within the Royal Gloucestershire, Berkshire & Wiltshire Regiment. Even further mergers, into 'The Rifles', face the regiment, where the sprit of 'The Springer's' will live on.

The great majority of photographs in this volume are held in the Royal Gloucestershire, Berkshire & Wiltshire Regimental archive at the Regimental Museum, The Wardrobe, Salisbury, Wiltshire, and are reproduced with the permission of the Regimental Museum Trustees. This is not intended to be a history of the regiment, but rather a selection of pictures from the Regimental archives that have been deposited over many years. Until now, they have remained unseen by old soldiers and members of the public alike; now, through publication, the story can live on.

Thanks to Len Webb, Len Pettit, Catherine Hemmings, Robert Stone, Don Briggs, Bert Fairchild, Doug Mortimer, 'Ozzie' Osbourne, Will Bennett, Lt-Col. (rtd) Ridley, Lt-Col. (rtd) Carter, Stan Dunn, Imperial War Museum, Australian War memorial. The Regimental Museum volunteers, Richard Long-Fox whose meticulous cataloguing has made the whole process much easier, Sue Johnson who has 'smoothed off the edges' of the written word, John Peters the ex-Museum Curator whose advice and guidance on regimental matters has been invaluable, and last but not least the Museum Curator Lt-Col. (rtd) David Chilton, whose continuing support and trust has made the whole project come alive.

M. McIntyre

The Royal Gloucestershire, Berkshire & Wiltshire Regimental Museum (Salisbury)
The Wardrobe, 58 The Close, Salisbury, SP1 2EX
Tel: (+44) 01722 419419
www.thewardrobe.org.uk

one

The First World War

The 1st Battalion, near Hungerford, Berkshire, en route back to their Barracks at Tidworth, *c.*1914. The Wiltshires, like all infantry battalions at this time, took great pride in marching long distances with the minimum of men falling out. On 13 August 1914, they embarked for France. By 26 August they were on the 'Retreat from Mons' where the training they received in England stood them in good stead. The officers in this photograph are still carrying swords, but soon after arrival in France they were discarded as impractical.

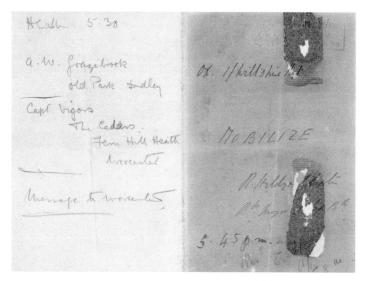

This insignificant looking piece of paper is among the most treasured possessions of the regiment. Although not unexpected, the arrival of the mobilisation notice on 4 August 1914 threw the 1st Battalion into the turmoil of the First World War. It was sent by runner to Lt-Col. A. W. Hasted, then commanding the battalion at Tidworth, who noted on it the time it was received. The 2nd Battalion was in Gibraltar when it received its mobilisation notice. It remained there for a few more weeks until it was relieved, then embarked for Europe. Landing in France on 7 October, the 2nd Battalion joined the 7th Division. By the time of the armistice on 11 November 1918, the Wiltshire Regiment had amassed fifty-nine Battle Honours, and a total of 4,924 officers and men had been Killed in Action or died of wounds.

The 2nd Battalion left England on 5 October 1914, and was 1,100 strong. After its heroic stand at Reutel near Ypres between 20–24 October, there were only two officers and 254 other ranks available for duty. Their hastily dug trenches were destroyed, and rifles developed major problems due to damage from days of continuous rapid fire, and by dirt and sand. This photograph, taken on or about 28 October, shows survivors of the 2nd Battalion re-grouping in the ramparts at Ypres that today flank the Menin Memorial Gate. These men are all regular soldiers, busy concentrating on getting their weapons back into good working order; a week later they needed them once again. If the 7th Division had not held this ground near Ypres, the way to the Channel ports would have been open and the course of the war would been very different.

A cartoon entitled 'Language-Kultur' from the magazine *Punch*, 16 December 1914. The caption reads, 'Voice from the Germans. "Doand shood Doand Shood, Ve vos de Viltshires"'. Whether a strong Wiltshire accent would have been intelligible to the Germans is another matter. Some personal diaries from this period recount how officers with the Wiltshire Battalions had difficulty in understanding their own men!

Members of the 1st Battalion on stand-by in an early trench system at the start of the war. This photograph is believed to be of the Kemmel area. These are all experienced soldiers who were well trained and knew how to handle their weapons. They have very little protection from the elements, except a greatcoat that soaked up more moisture than it kept out. The War Diary of the 1st Battalion records, 'Some trenches have to be built almost entirely of sandbags. Communication trenches almost invariably get full of water, and for the most part are not practicable'. At this time, very few days went by when men were not killed or wounded by snipers and sporadic shell fire.

Believed to have been taken in late 1914, this photograph sums up the spirit of the regiment at that time. These men have fought the German Army to a standstill, suffering considerable casualties in the process. By the end of the year, the 1st Battalion had lost twenty-six officers and 1,000 men since its arrival in France. The replacements at this time were all experienced soldiers recalled to the Colours. Though out of condition by Army standards, they knew how to handle their weapons after their years of previous practice. Fifteen well-aimed shots a minute was the expectation, sometimes referred to by these old soldiers as 'the mad minute'.

No. 10 Platoon, 'C' Company, 1st Battalion in trench 'J2' at Kemmel, Belgium, December 1914. It is believed that this photograph was taken around 25 December. The soldiers were starting to adapt to the conditions, using whatever was available, such as sandbags inside greatcoats to keep out the cold. The War Diary for 25 December 1914 reads, 'In trenches, a thick fog all day. Practically no shelling on either side, but a little sniping in the trenches. Owing to moonlight a good deal of difficulty in relieving fire trenches. Cold'. They did not take part in the Christmas truce. On Christmas Day the battalion had two men killed, one wounded and one missing.

A different view of the same trench system. Both photographs are believed to have been taken by Captain Cary Barnard. The 1st Battalion had gone into the trenches in front of Kemmel on 30 November 1914. For almost four months, until 11 March 1915, they spent four days resting at Locre and four days in the front line on duty in the Kemmel trenches. These men later became known as 'The Old Contemptibles' – by the end of the war very few were left. While these regular soldiers held the line in France, the Territorial Battalions were mobilising and the 'Kitchener' service battalions were in training. Although no major battles were fought in the area, by the end of January 1915 a total of eighteen members of the battalion had been killed and sixteen wounded.

Recruits for the 1st/4th Battalion marching through Trowbridge, *c.*1914. The 4th Battalion were on Annual Camp at Sling Plantation, Bulford, on Salisbury Plain in August 1914 when the order came to mobilise. Drafts from the Depot at Trowbridge quickly brought the battalion to well over strength, and the decision was taken to form a new battalion. The original battalion became 1st/4th, and the new one the 2nd/4th. The 1st/4th recruits seen here are all volunteers, some already kitted out in khaki uniform. In October the 1st/4th sailed for India to relieve a regular unit, followed shortly after by the 2nd/4th.

The advance party of the 5th Battalion, on Cirencester Railway Station, 14 December 1914. The 5th (Service) Battalion was formed in Tidworth in August 1914. Quickly reaching a total of 2,000 men, it was, like the 4th, split into two, with the new unit becoming the 6th Battalion. All the sergeants in this photograph are regular soldiers of the Wiltshire Regiment or recalled reservists with recent service. From left to right: 2nd/Lts H. Belcher; H.B.L. Braund; F. Priestley; E.R. Troward. Lt Belcher was later Killed in Action in Gallipoli on 7 August 1915, and Lt Priestley was Killed in Action on 27 May 1918 while serving in the 1st Battalion. He had been awarded the Military Cross and reached the rank of captain.

Soldiers of the 5th (Service) Battalion form up upon arrival at Cirencester Railway Station, 14 December 1914. The sergeant to the front was a regular soldier; those behind him were all volunteers. Seven months later, this battalion sailed for Gallipoli, where it was involved in a number of actions. On 10 August 1915, together with the 6th North Lancashire Regiment, they were overwhelmed by a Turkish attack at Sari Bair. A survivor from the 5th Battalion later remembered that the Turks, 'came in a monstrous mass, packed shoulder to shoulder, in some places eight deep. Practically all their first line was shot by our men, practically all the second line were bayoneted, but the third line got into our trenches, and overwhelmed the garrison, after taking the second line trenches they destroyed the 5th Wiltshire Regiment almost to a man'.

The Machine Gun Section, 5th Battalion, Inkerman Barracks, Woking, Surrey, in 1915, before sailing for Gallipoli. At this time the battalion was issued with two Vickers machine guns. Later in the war, the machine gun teams were grouped together in the newly created Machine Gun Corps. From left to right, second row: –?–, –?–, Lt A. Huckett, Lt J. Bush, Sgt J. Axford, –?–, –?–. Lt Huckett was Killed in Action on 10 August at Gallipoli, and is commemorated on the Helles Memorial.

ORIGINALLY PRINTED FOR THE 6TH SERVICE BTN FORMED AT TIDWORTH SEPT 1914 UNDER THE COMMAND OF COL: JEFFERIES.

**For gootness sake Halt!
der 6th WILTS.
are koming.**

The 6th (Service) Battalion were formed at Tidworth in September 1914 under the command of Lt-Col. A.G. Jefferies, a regular officer who recently commanded the 2nd Battalion. At first they did not have any uniforms and Regimental Sgt-Maj. Wickins, also late of the 2nd Battalion, always wore a bowler hat on parade. One third of the battalion came from Wiltshire, a third were London Cockneys, and a third were from Birmingham. Lt-Col. Jefferies was very keen to get his battalion fit for war and the training was hard. The 6th Battalion went to France as part of the 19th Division in July 1915, and remained on the Western Front throughout the First World War. They were disbanded in Devizes in 1919. This postcard was one of many similar items produced at the time, each customised to represent a particular unit.

Two members of the 6th (Service) Battalion training at either Basingstoke or Weston-super-Mare, c.1915. They are practising using the field telephone with one soldier listening for the message and dictating it to his comrade. The repair of telephone lines broken by shellfire cost many lives. Both these soldiers are qualified signallers as denoted by their trade badges of 'crossed flags' on their left forearms. Signallers also had to master the use of flags – the handle of one can be seen leaning against the wall. However, the use of signalling flags on the Western Front quickly fell into disuse due to the obvious dangers.

The 7th (Service) Battalion (nicknamed the 'The Shiny Seventh') in Devizes, Market Place, March 1915, five months before they embarked for Greece. The battalion marched to Devizes from Marlborough, returning later the same day, a round trip of about thirty miles. On the grey horse is the Adjutant Lt L. Fairchild. Lt-Col. Walter Rocke, the commanding officer (mounted), was known to his men as 'Old Bonny'. He quickly injected the spirit of the Wiltshire Regiment into this fledgling battalion.

Recruiting in the villages of Wiltshire. Lt-Col. Rocke mounted an aggressive recruiting campaign throughout the county. Here we seen band members and the recruiting sergeant of the 7th Battalion in Hullavington, *c.*1915, 'Questioning' a young carter. It appears to be an unequal contest with four against one. At this time the Army relied on volunteers, as conscription was not brought in until 1916.

The band of the 7th Battalion enter the village of Sherston, *c.*1915. The battalion acquired the band instruments after Lt-Col. Rocke made a successful appeal in the *Daily Telegraph*. Many of the bandsmen had gained their musical experience playing in their local brass bands. Headed by Sgt-Maj. Parfitt and Sgt Wotton, the band has attracted many juvenile followers. Some of the youngsters may well have joined the Wiltshire Regiment in future years.

The band of the 7th Battalion marching through the village of Hullavington, being watched by interested local farm labourers, *c.*1915. Life in the country was tough so the rigours of Army life would not be a great shock for such men. One of the factors which deterred the young men in these villages from joining up immediately was harvesting. As this was labour intensive, it could not have happened without them. Many did later join the Army, as an examination of the number of names on local Wiltshire war memorials will testify.

A recruiting sergeant of the 7th Battalion in a North Wiltshire village, no doubt trying to persuade the lady that her husband should join the regiment, *c.*1915. The old tradition of the recruiting staff wearing a rosette on the side of the cap was resurrected by the commanding officer, Lt-Col. Rocke. The 7th Battalion trained hard until September 1915, when it embarked for France. After two months in the trenches came a move to Salonika.

General Wilson inspecting a Guard of Honour of the 7th Battalion in Salonika. Every soldier in this guard is 6ft or over. The battalion reached Salonika on 21 November 1915. The early days there consisted mainly of the construction of defences. There were a number of minor (by Western Front standards) actions and the ever-present threat of malaria. On 24 April 1917 the battalion was involved in the assault on the Grand Couronne, which resulted in the loss of 300 other ranks and all but one of the fifteen officers who took part becoming casualties. The Regimental history recorded that several of the Wiltshire companies were eventually commanded by warrant officers and sergeants, like those of the 62nd (Wiltshire) Regiment of Foot, their predecessors, at the Battle of Ferozeshah in India in 1845. The battalion remained in Salonika until July 1918, then returned to France to take part in the final battles on the Western Front.

The Machine Gun Section of the 7th Battalion take part in a brigade competition arranged by the battalion in Salonika, *c.*1915. On the battalion's arrival in Salonika, they had to master the use of mules to carry the heavy machine guns and equipment over the local mountainous terrain. (IWM)

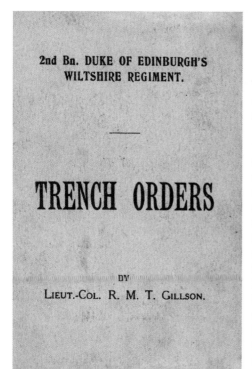

2nd Bn. DUKE OF EDINBURGH'S WILTSHIRE REGIMENT.

TRENCH ORDERS

BY
LIEUT.-COL. R. M. T. GILLSON.

Trench orders issued by Lt-Col. RMT Gillson, the commanding officer of the 2nd Battalion, 1916. The first page inside reads:

1. A Regiment should guard its trenches as closely as it guards its honour and its good name, and rather than surrender a foot to the enemy every officer, non-commissioned officer or private must be prepared to die in them.
2. The word 'Retire' is never to be heard in a trench.
3. If in spite of every effort put forward to repel the enemy, he should still succeed in gaining a footing in the trenches, a counter attack will be immediately launched against the lost portion of the trench. This, if delivered immediately and with dash, is bound to succeed. With this object in view, the company bombers should, as a rule, be distributed along the line held by the company in tactical units, i.e. sections or sub sections, so that sufficient numbers may be near at hand to bomb an intruder out.

The 1st Battalion on the Western Front, 28 June 1916. At this time the battalion was carrying out an extensive training programme, and on the 28th made a night march to Puchevillers. This photograph is believed to show the start of that march. These are fully equipped infantry soldiers, carrying everything necessary to maintain their fighting capability in the trenches, in loads weighing up to 80lb.

The 1st Battalion advance during an attack at Leipzig Redoubt, Thiepval, August 1916. This photograph by Ernest Brooks is believed to show a live attack. Brooks is clearly operating his camera from behind a trench parapet, which is visible in the foreground. The battalion made two attacks, one on 21 August with two companies, and the second on the 24th with the whole battalion. Brigade Major Johnson later recalled:

> Two companies of the 1st Wilts got out of their trenches, lined up for the assault, and pushed out their snipers in front into crump holes from which they shot at any German who ventured to look over. As the barrage lifted the 1st Wilts charged over, as a matter of fact they started a bit too soon and actually stopped and stood up in No Mans Land until the barrage lifted. That men should stand quietly in the middle of No Mans Land like this showed that they were well in hand and well disciplined. (IWM)

A platoon of the 1st Battalion, 16 August 1916, shortly after the battles at Thiepval. The platoon commander is sat second from the left. All are armed with the Lee Enfield .303 rifle. One of the battalion's twenty-four Lewis light machine guns (with its ammunition drum removed) can be seen in the foreground. After the actions at Thiepval, in which the battalion sustained 320 casualties, it made its way to Bouzincourt for rest, reorganisation and training. (IWM)

This photograph is believed to have been taken at Bouzincourt in August 1916. It shows the 1st Battalion marching back with some 'Trophies of War'. Nearly all are wearing captured German equipment, helmets and clothing. It appears that their morale is high, no doubt helped by reports of their actions at the Leipzig Salient in the national newspapers. These had headlines like, 'Wilts and Worcesters defeat the Prussian guard'. (IWM)

A closer view of the same group. The soldier on the right brandishing a German stick grenade is a sergeant major. The battalion 'joker' in the centre is modelling a 'liberated' German greatcoat and cap, with several other soldiers wearing captured Pickelhauben. These ornate items of headgear were much prized and many changed hands behind the lines for considerable sums of money. Some eventually made their way into the Regimental Museum. (IWM)

The same group of soldiers from the 1st Battalion at Bouzincourt. The battalion remained at this location for about a week, carrying out extensive training. On 2 September 1916 it once again went into the front line and attacked the German trenches. There was heavy enemy machine gun fire, but even more casualties were caused by what is today termed 'friendly fire'. (IWM)

While the 1st, 2nd and 6th Battalions fought on the Western Front, the 1st/4th were in India. From November 1914 to September 1917, there were numerous 'Flag Marches' which had the effect of moulding the battalion into a cohesive unit. Here we see the camel transport used by the battalion during one of these marches.

In September 1917 the 1st/4th embarked for Palestine for active service. Prior to that date, drafts from the battalion were sent to other units in the Persian Gulf. Once the 1st/4th had arrived in Palestine, these soldiers rejoined the battalion. Here we see L/Cpl Mackett, Ptes Gaiton, Cosser, Ruddle, Goth and Preen, the first draft from 'B' Company, July 1915. Three of these men were Killed in Action in 1917: Pte Preen on 12 February, Pte Cosser on 22 May and L/Cpl Mackett on 7 November.

Right: All Wiltshire Regiment battalions were nicknamed 'The Moonrakers' after the famous Wiltshire legend (see page 7). This First World War postcard shows a Wiltshire soldier raking from the sky a moon bearing an image of the Kaiser. Stonehenge is visible in the background.

Below: The 'Moonrakers', the concert troupe of the 1st/4th Battalion in India, *c.*1916. Of the twenty-three soldiers who presented themselves for audition, nine were chosen to form the troupe. These were 2nd/Lt Tucker; L/Cpls Inglis and Brown; Ptes Caines, Carter, Edwards, Golding, Mattock and Shore. Their most notable song was 'Patty' by Pte Shore, which included the words 'patty packs all things together, so the tummies can't tell whether it is pants, preserves or pickles, pretty polly packs'. The 'Moonrakers' provided entertainment for both the garrison and the battalion in India up until the time they embarked for Palestine in 1917, after which they had a more pressing engagement with the Turkish Army.

THE WILTSHIRE REGIMENT
" THE MOONRAKERS "

Soldiers of the 1st/4th Battalion stand guard over mutineers in Delhi Fort, March 1917. The battalion garrisoned the fort just prior to embarking on active service. A number of soldiers from the 7th Rajput Regiment mutinied, which resulted in two members of that regiment facing court martial. The prisoner pictured here tried to escape twice, letting himself down the fort wall by using his turban as an escape rope. After the court martial the sentences of the court were read out to the whole Delhi Garrison. One soldier was deported for life and the potential escapee was hanged.

A platoon of the 5th Battalion in Mesopotamia, having arrived from Port Said following the evacuation from Gallipoli, *c.*1916. The battalion was so depleted by the battles on the Gallipoli peninsula that 750 reinforcements were needed. Once up to strength the battalion went to Basra, and then continued up the Tigris in barges to Amara. The 5th Battalion fought the Turks on this axis for the next two and a half years. In this photograph the regimental helmet flashes (the cross pattée) can be seen.

Above left: The 1st/4th Battalion in 1917. In November of this year the battalion went into the trenches south of Turkish-held Gaza, taking up positions at Queens' Redoubt and Lees Hill. In this photograph, taken by Lt Viscount Folkstone, we see Sgt Frederick Mundy (nearest camera) and Lt Merewether. On the side of the trench is an empty shellcase which was to be rung like a bell in the event of a gas attack (it was never used). Sgt Mundy went on to win a Distinguished Conduct Medal. Lt Merewether was wounded in his spine on 13 November 1917 during the assault on El Mesmiyeh, and died in Port Said on 20 December.

Above right: The wounded of the 1st/4th Battalion in the monastery at Kuryet-El-Enab, 21 November 1917. The photographer is believed to be Lord Folkstone. The position had been taken after a bayonet charge by the 1st/4th and the Gurkhas. Sgt Couldrey, who had earlier won the Distinguished Conduct Medal for his actions at El Mesmiyeh on 13 November 1917, recalled what happened next:

> While we were putting on our packs ready to move off again I heard a terrific bang which deafened me. One of 'Johnnys' shells had pitched right near us and I heard a lot of groans, and turning round saw Charlie Read go down, Charlie Badder had his knee blown away, L/Cpl Hawkins was hit in the stomach. Then I looked at myself and saw my right hand was bleeding terribly and had a piece of shell stuck in. Pte Newman had both legs hit badly and one eye blown away, Pte Smith had his leg damaged, Pte Chivers lay as still as a post, Lord Folkstone was hobbling around with his foot damaged and five Mules which carried the Lewis Guns were killed.

Following the shelling the monastery became a temporary dressing station while the battalion moved on. The wounded, including Sgt Couldrey, were sent down the line to hospital. L/Cpl Hawkins, Ptes Read, Badder, Chivers and Parsons were killed in the incident, a fact which seems to have been omitted by the Regimental history, which stated, 'the 1st/4th had only 34 wounded'. (IWM)

The 1st/4th Battalion in Palestine. This photograph is believed to have been taken shortly after a downpour in December 1917 in the vicinity of Ramaleh. It shows the Quartermaster's limbers taking up rations to the front line. In command (seated left) is RQMS Bernard Carter. The commanding officer, Lt-Col. Armstrong, later remembered, 'It rained most of the way and the track was a sea of mud, our limbers were up to their axles in the mud in places and the camels kept sliding about anyhow, the limbers arrived at 23.00 hours. Sgt Henley, the master cook was, as usual splendid, so was Pte Baily 'D' Company cook'. The battalion spent three weeks in the Ramaleh area and was there when the Turks surrendered Jerusalem on 9 December 1917.

The reserve company 1st/4th Battalion, Berukin, August 1918. The battalion had taken over this position from the 1/123 Rifles (Indian Army) on 9 July, and remained there until 23 August. The battalion was heavily reinforced by soldiers from the 2nd/5th Hampshire Regiment, with all the companies rotating between Berukin and Toogood Hill. Patrols were sent out every night. The Regimental history later recalled, 'Flies and dirt produced dysentery, and rocks and sand difficult conditions for digging trenches'. One more major action was fought at El Tireh, where the commanding officer, Lt-Col. Armstrong, was killed. At the end of the war the battalion moved to Kantara on the Suez Canal, and in January 1919, to Port Said. The much reduced regiment reached Trowbridge in October 1919. The battalion earned for the regiment the following battle honours: Gaza, Nebi Samwil, Jerusalem, Megiddo, Sharon and Palestine 1917–18.

The 1st Battalion on parade at Esquerdes which lies five miles (8km) south-west of St Omer, France, 15 May 1917. The battalion spent eight days here training for the battle of Messines that was due to start the following month. On 16 May they carried out a practice attack on similar terrain well behind the lines. The commanding officer had seventeen points that were known by heart by the men who were to take part in the attack. The five main points were:

1. Men must anticipate a counter attack.
2. Men must not stop to attend to wounded.
3. If a nest of machine guns is encountered, or any strong point, it must be dealt with at once.
4. Beware of people dressed as staff officers.
5. There is no such word as 'Retire'.

The officers of the 1st Battalion, Esquerdes, May 1917. From left to right, back row:
2nd/Lt G. Atkinson; Lt W. Holmes; Capt. G. Brown, MC; Capt. J Taylor MC; Maj. S. Ogilvie, DSO;
Lt-Col. A. Williams; Capt. R. Hayward, MC; Capt G. Russell, DSO; Lt W. Rowe; 2nd/Lt S. Jones;
2nd/Lt T. Smith; Capt. I. Gingell; 2nd/Lt D. Brown; Lt H. Webber. Centre row: 2nd/Lt Tanner,
MC; The Padre; Lt H. Turner; 2nd/Lt D. Hannam; Lt Fowler; 2nd/Lt H. Brown; Lt N. King;
2nd/Lt W. Ludford; Lt D. Jeans; 2nd/Lt W. Bidwell; 2nd/Lt G. Hillings. Front row:
2nd/Lt R. Swayne, MC; Lt E. Hill; The medical officer; 2nd/Lt E. Parsons, MC; 2nd/Lt S. Terry;
Lt C. Sainsbury, MC; 2nd/Lt G. Clarkson; 2nd/Lt A. Parsons. Lying down: 2nd/Lt C. Thomas;
2nd/Lt G. Filor. Capt. Hayward later went on to win the Victoria Cross.

Right: The Wiltshire Regiment banner displayed at the choral commemoration of the First Seven Divisions at the Royal Albert Hall, 15 December 1917. In 1914 the 1st Battalion had become part of the 3rd Division, while the 2nd Battalion was in the 7th Division. The invitation from the national organising committee said, 'My committee hope that the Wiltshire Regiment will do us the honour of sending four officers and eight non commissioned officers and men of their veterans of 1914, to occupy a box set aside for your Regiment'. What became of the banner is not known.

Below: Three experienced soldiers of the Wiltshire Regiment demonstrate the type of equipment worn in 1918. It continued in use until 1937 when the 37-pattern webbing was introduced. The men shown are in 'fighting order'. On the left is a sergeant major and right, two private soldiers, both wearing two long service stripes on their left lower arm, indicating six years' service. The man on the right has two wound stripes. The soldiers left and right have their box respirators at the 'ready' position, while the one in the centre is wearing his. He stands with bayonet fixed, and in the 'en garde' position.

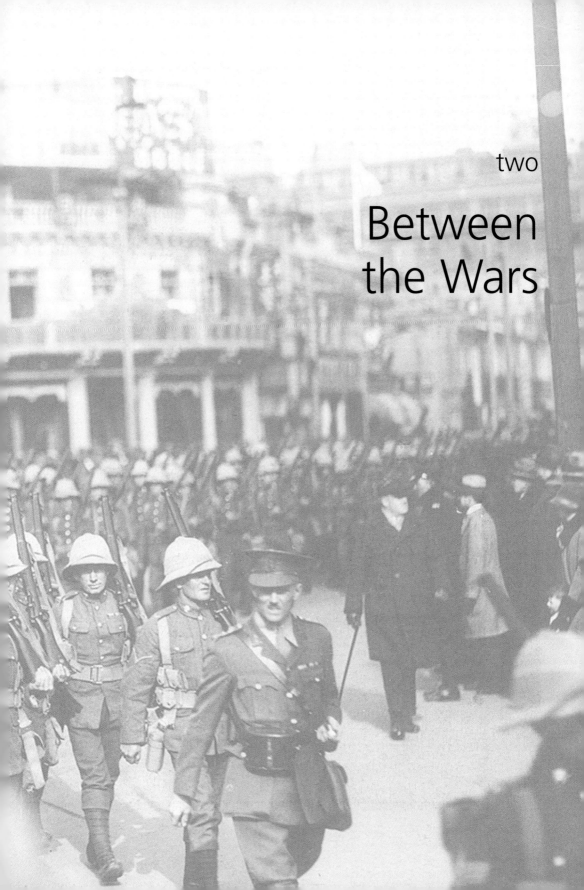

two

Between
the Wars

The Market Place, Salisbury, 6 June 1919. The Colour party of the 1st Battalion approaches waiting city councillors. Two weeks earlier, the 2nd Battalion had taken part in the city's Empire Day celebrations. At the end of the First World War, both battalions demobilised in France before returning to England in 1919. The remaining small nucleus of regular soldiers reorganised before their next postings; the 1st Battalion at the Regimental Depot in Devizes and the 2nd Battalion at Chiseldon, near Swindon. The 1st Battalion then went to Ireland and the 2nd to Hong Kong.

In 1919 a detachment of 200 regular soldiers from the Wiltshire Regiment under the command of Capt. Ponsford, MC, formed part of the Russian Relief Force. Members of a composite 'Hampshire' Battalion, their role was to protect British interests in Archangel and Murmansk during the Russian Revolution. They fought for a time against the Bolsheviks until the collapse of the White Russians led to their evacuation and return to England. Second row starting eighth from left: Lt Skiggs and on his left Lt Rimmer; Capt. Sabben; Major Ponsford, MC; Lt Ludford; Lt Filor, MC, DCM; Lt Auton, MC and Bar, DCM. Lt Auton won the bar to his Military Cross in Russia, and the citation reads.

> During the enemy attack on Bolshe-Ozerki on 1st September 1919 he was commanding the forward post four versts [a verst is a Russian measurement equaling about two thirds of a mile] from Bolshe-Ozerki with one platoon as garrison. This post withstood the attack of at least 300 men thanks to his gallant and able leadership, though the enemy attacked on three sides at once for a space of two hours. The enemy finally withdrew.

The village of Troitsa in Russia, captured by the British forces and used as a base by the Wiltshires of 'Z' Company, and as the 'Hampshire' Battalion headquarters. At a battalion sports day held there, the Wiltshire contingent won the Guard Mounting and Tug-o-War competitions. From this position, 'Z' Company occupied blockhouses astride the railway to Vologa where Lt Auton's platoon engaged the 'Bolos' [Bolsheviks]. Two soldiers from his platoon won the Military Medal (Sgts Jefferies and Pinnock) and Pvt Jasper won the Distinguished Conduct Medal, the citation reading:

> For fine courage at Bolshe-Ozerki on 1 September 1919. He was sent out to cut the communication and line of retreat of the attacking force. He killed the entire crew of a Bolo Lewis gun, capturing the gun. He was eventually wounded, but remained on duty, and when the Bolos again attacked he killed three more and wounded several more. He did magnificent work.

Right: The 'Hampshire' Battalion returned from Russia on 6 October 1919 and went to Crowborough, where its members were dispersed to their own Regiments, 'Z' Company rejoining the 1st Battalion Wiltshire Regiment in Dublin. Before leaving the camp, many of the soldiers sat for commemorative photographs. This one shows CSMs Yeats, Robbins, Moss, Waite, MC, DCM; and Bramstt, CQMS Archard and Sgt Drummer Porter. CSM Waite is seated in the centre row on the right. On his left lower sleeve are three wound stripes. On his left upper arm is the White star which was worn by all units serving in the North Russian Expedition.

On 21 November 1920, the Irish Finance Minister and head of the Irish republican brotherhood, Michael Collins, ordered the assassination of what was known as the 'Cairo Gang', fourteen high-ranking British Intelligence officers sent to infiltrate Irish nationalist organisations. Early that morning, all fourteen were killed – a number of them in their own homes, and in some cases with their family in close proximity. This action severely crippled British intelligence operations in Ireland and caused consternation among Crown forces. Here we see the band of the 1st Battalion with side drums draped in black at the head of the funeral procession, turning into Park Street on their long journey to North Wall Quay in Dublin, from where the remains of the deceased officers were repatriated to England. The soldiers at the head of the procession are marching with their arms reversed.

Dublin, 1922. The 1st Battalion were stationed in Palace Barracks, in the heart of the city. On 14 April 1922 the Four Courts building next to the barracks was taken by Rory O'Connor, and the Wiltshires found themselves bystanders as the Nationalist Army and the IRA fought for supremacy. After a period of inaction, the new Army fired on their former comrades in the Four Courts and the Irish Civil War began in earnest. On 30 June an enormous explosion occurred in the Records Office. A towering mushroom cloud rose 200ft over the Four Courts and the remains of records from as early as the twelfth century rained down upon the city. Miraculously, no one was killed, although forty members of the storming party were badly injured. Additional explosions, intentionally set or otherwise, occurred during the day. The battalion were on full alert at this time and the event was captured by a Wiltshire Regiment officer who was on the belfry roof of the barracks with his camera.

The 1st Battalion Football Team, Aldershot, 1922. In the presence of George V the team beat the Royal Welch Fusiliers 3-1 to become the Army Football Champions, 1921–22. Standing just behind the King, introducing the players is Capt. K Oliphant, MC. The King is shaking hands with the goalkeeper, Pte P. Topp. The other players were CQMS J. Fortune; Sgt E. Poolman, MM; CSM A. Baish; L/Cpl E. Veck, MM; CSM H. Wilkins; Sgt C. Giles (Team Capt.); Cpl R. Monk; Pte G. Thomas; L/Cpl A. Ballinger. After the battalion moved to Tidworth, their footballing success continued when they again won the Army Cup 1923-24, this time beating the Royal Artillery 1-0.

The 1st Battalion's three years in Dublin produced many sporting triumphs, and not just on the football field. Its teams also became military champions in Athletics, Cross-Country Running, Tug-of-War and Bayonet Fighting. Here we see the winners of the Irish Command Bayonet Tournament, 1922. Seated: –?–; Capt. Hayward, VC, MC; Lt-Col. Dansey, CMG, DSO; –?–; –?–.

Royal Barracks, Dublin, 17 December 1922. The 1st Battalion form up on the parade square prior to marching out for the last time when they handed over to troops of the Irish Free State. The *Irish Times* recorded:

> In the Royal Barracks Captain P. Murphy, National Army, took over from Colonel Gillson DSO, Commanding the Wiltshire Regiment. With Col. Gillson were Captains Oliphant, Lloyd and Oldfield of the same regiment. The Irish troops, who had marched from GHQ after taking over there, lined up at one side of the square of the Royal Barracks. The British troops (Wiltshire Regiment) faced them. Green uniforms and Khaki faced each other in that grey, stark square. And then the Colour Guard of the 'Wilts' brought them into position in the ranks, with the band playing the regimental march 'The Lincolnshire Poacher'. The Free State Troops saluted the Colours as they were carried past, and the officers of the British regiment returned the compliment with the order 'Eyes right' as they passed.

In 1932 the 1st Battalion were in Shanghai with the Lincolnshire Regiment, who claimed the Regimental march 'The Lincolnshire Poacher' as their own. The Wiltshires then reverted to 'The Vly', which had been officially sanctioned in March 1881.

At 3.10 p.m. on 17 December 1922, the *Arviona* left Dublin bound for England. She carried the 1st Battalion which was one of the last British battalions to leave Ireland. The battalion's destination was Tidworth, its home for the next three years.

A postcard purchased at embarkation points by generations of soldiers on their way to India for a tour of duty. The regimental cap badge was adjusted to reflect whichever regiment was going abroad, in this case the 2nd Battalion Wiltshire Regiment, which went to Bangalore in 1922. Soldiers of the 1st Battalion would have sent similar cards in 1936 when they were stationed there.

Soldiers of the 2nd Battalion on a route march in India, *c.*1923. Route marches on the Indian sub-continent always started early to avoid the heat of the day. The normal routine was fifty minutes' marching followed by ten minutes' rest. The battalion was normally headed by the Corps of Drums, who would play it into villages and towns. The sight of a British battalion 'On the March' in India was summed up by Kipling:

> We're marchin' on relief over Injia's coral strand,
> Eight 'undred fightin' Englishmen, the Colonel, and the Band;
> Ho! get away you bullock-man, you've 'eard the bugle blowed,
> There's a regiment a-comin' down the Grand Trunk Road;
> With its best foot first
> And the road a-sliding past,
> An' every bloomin' campin'-ground exactly like the last;
> While the Big Drum says,
> With 'is 'rowdy-dowdy-dow!'–
> 'Kiko kissywarsti - don't you - hamsher argy jow'

The warrant officers and sergeants of 'B' Company, 2nd Battalion, Bangalore, India, 1923. These men are all experienced soldiers with no less than five wearing the 1914 Star with clasp, otherwise known as 'The Mons Star'. From left to right, back row: Sgts Gorton; Dawes; Campbell, DCM; Minty. From left to right, middle row: Sgt Arthur; CSM Buckland; CQMS Bayerstock; Sgt Whitbread. From left to right, front row: Sgt Prior; L/Sgt Baggs. Sgt Campbell won his Distinguished Conduct Medal on 8 October 1918 during an attack by the 1st Battalion on German positions east of Montecouvez Farm in France, when he took command of his platoon after his officer was killed. Sgt Minty went with the battalion to Shanghai in 1929 where he died. His son followed him into the regiment.

THE BEER SHIFTERS, SAVAGE SQUAD, BOXING DAY, INDIA 1922.

Soldiers of the 2nd Battalion, Bangalore, India, Boxing Day, 1922. Unless soldiers were on guard duty they were very much left to their own devices, and those who were not members of the Army Temperance Society tended to consume copious amounts of beer in the 'Wet Canteen'. Here we see the 'Beer Shifters Savage Squad' in action.

The 1st Battalion march into Shanghai in 1932, having arrived from Egypt on the troopship *Lancashire*. At the time there was considerable disturbance in Shanghai owing to the Sino-Japanese war. Here we see the battalion after a seven-mile march from the docks to the racecourse, accompanied by armoured cars of the Shanghai Light Horse. The pavements on either side were lined with thousands of Chinese, who appeared far more interested in the Wiltshires' arrival than in the battle which was raging in other parts of the city. A War Diary was opened and the battalion went onto a war footing, spending a significant amount of time on outpost duty. Its role was to protect the European settlements.

Soldiers resting shortly after arrival. The man on the right is doing what infantrymen learn quickly – 'sleep when you can'. The battalion's duties included checkpoints, patrolling, manning outposts (at any one time over 200 men were on outpost duty) and internal security within the settlement, enforcing a curfew. Shanghai Area order No.9 received by the battalion stated, 'The use of batons to be discontinued, troops called out to quell a riot to use the weapons with which they are armed. No greater force to be used than necessary. Rifle and bayonet to be used in sequence (a) the butt, (b) the bayonet, (c) fire. Automatic weapons to be used only if other means fail'.

A section from the 1st Battalion on the Western perimeter 'Standing to', rifles at the ready and with bayonets fixed. Although the Japanese and Chinese were no direct threat to British forces, the battalion adopted a high profile to send a clear message to potential aggressors that they would be met with considerable force. The War Diary records that the battalion immediately set about improving the defensive system which was in a very rudimentary state, and patrolling the area in force in order to 'dominate' the ground. The soldiers from the battalion worked very hard to get the defences secure, at the same time ensuring their living conditions were reasonably habitable – their achievement is clearly shown by this photograph.

The 1st Battalion War Diary records:

> The posts taken over were in the form of breast-works of sandbags in some cases and earthworks combined with sandbags in others. The former type were to be found on road junctions, and the latter on the embankment. One section of the Machine gunners, at No.14 post occupied on old house using the windows reinforced by sandbags as loopholes. Posts were constructed for all round defence.

Here we see the reference to the machine-gun post. Later generations of soldiers in the Duke of Edinburgh's Royal Regiment who served in Northern Ireland would be very familiar with the routine. The battalion spent ten months in Shanghai, after which they went to Malaya.

The 2nd Battalion, Palestine, 1936 or '37. The battalion was part of the 1st Division and was based at Sarafand, near Lydda. Most of the time was taken up with patrols, guard duties and raids. Following a busy first month on Internal Security duties due to an Arab strike, the situation calmed down. Shortly after their arrival in Palestine, members of 'A' Company came under sniper fire at an isolated outpost at Nes Siona, fortunately with no casualties. Here we see a well-armed mobile patrol group about to embark on patrol.

Suicide Squad Palestine 36 – 37.

Patrolling when deployed on Internal Security operations can be rather boring, but is a vital tactic to disrupt terrorist movements. In this case, the tedium of foot patrols and guard duties was alleviated by the use of the motor rail cars at Majdal, Palestine. A local initiative designed to give the troops more flexibility, it was, in effect, a motor vehicle adapted to operate on the railway line. Here we see a patrol of the 2nd Battalion receiving an inspection from General Wavell, prior to the start of one of these patrols.

Soldiers of the 2nd Battalion stand guard while Royal Engineers prepare a house for demolition at El Mughar. The battalion worked closely with the Palestine Police, assisting when occupants were identified for arrest, after which their homes would be blown up.

Soldiers of the 2nd Battalion 'sangar building' in the hills in Palestine, 1936–37. A sangar is a rock-built emplacement that provided cover from sniper and other types of small-arms fire. The old 'India hands' of the battalion would have been well versed in this skill, which was very necessary when the ground was too rocky for trenches. Soldiers who served here were entitled to wear the General Service Medal with clasp 'Palestine'. By the end of 1937 the battalion was back in Aldershot.

Above: The 1st Battalion arrived in Bangalore, India, from Singapore in 1936. They remained there until the outbreak of the Second World War. Here we see the battalion shortly after their arrival marching past on the King's Birthday Parade. The Colours seen behind the Second Company were carried for a further three years before being replaced.

Right: The 1st Battalion, Bangalore, India, Armistice Day 1938. The very elaborate wreath displays the battle honours of the 62nd (Wiltshire) Regiment from a previous era.

The battalion quickly fell into the routine of soldiering in India, where sport played a major role. There were many victories in shooting contests, and in successive years they beat two famous rugby regiments, The King's Own and The Gloucesters in the final of the Madras District competition.

'C' Company, 4th (Territorial) Battalion on church parade, Chippenham, April 1937. The battalion had a full corps of drums and band. The Territorials in Wiltshire were a thriving organisation and the 4th Battalion was fully manned in the years leading up to the Second World War. In July 1939 the battalion went to Exmouth for their annual camp; just two months later war broke out.

As the clouds of war developed over Europe the British Army continued training with the weapons available. Budgets were tight between the wars and the forces very much under-resourced. One exception was the introduction of a magazine fed, air cooled .303 light machine gun called the 'Bren gun'. It was to prove very reliable and with minor modifications it remained in service in the British Army until the introduction of the Light Support Weapon in the early 1980s. Here we see the senior officers of the 2nd Battalion on Bellerby ranges, Catterick, Yorkshire familiarising themselves with the newly issued weapon in 1939. Nearest the camera is the commanding officer, Lt-Col. Oliphant, MC. He had served in the Regiment in the First World War, was captured at Neuve Chapelle in 1915 and spent the rest of that war making repeated and determined efforts to escape.

three

March on
the Colours

In July 1919 peace celebrations were held by the Allies in London and Paris. In both cities, the 1st Battalion Colours were carried by Lt R. Hayward, VC, MC (on the left with the King's Colour), and Lt S. Parker, MC, DCM (right, with the Regimental Colour). In the centre is RSM Kepner, DCM and Bar. These Colours carried the pre-First World War Battle Honours. A Battle Honour is defined as, 'a public commemoration of a battle, action or engagement, of which not only past and present, but future generations of the Regiment can be proud.'

The Colours of the 2nd Battalion, seen here around 1926 in Kamptee, India, were presented by HRH The Duke of Edinburgh at Aldershot in 1871 and carried by the 99th Foot (later 2nd Wiltshires) through the Zulu Wars of 1879–80. These Colours were returned to England in 1926 and laid up in Salisbury Cathedral, where what remains of them can be seen to this day. From left to right: Drummer Darty; Sgt Drummer Porter; Drummer Busby.

In 1926 Field Marshal Lord Birdwood presented new Colours to the 2nd Battalion at Kamptee. Until after the First World War, the Regiment's Battle Honours appeared only on the Regimental Colour. Now with forty-seven new honours awarded for service in the First World War, revised regulations allowed for just ten of these to appear on the King's Colour (left). These Colours were carried by the battalion until 1948 when the 1st and 2nd Battalions amalgamated.

In 1908, as a result of the Territorial Forces Act, the 4th Battalion was formed from the 1st Wiltshire Rifle Volunteers and the 2nd Volunteer Battalion of the Wiltshire Regiment. The battalion received its first set of Colours at Leighton Camp, Westbury, on 3 August 1927. They were presented by Brig-Gen. The Earl of Radnor CIE, CBE, TD, ADC, Lord Lieutenant of Wiltshire and Hon. Col. of the 4th Battalion. The money needed to produce these Colours was raised by the Dowager Countess of Pembroke and the Countess of Radnor, assisted by many well-known Wiltshire ladies. Kneeling down, waiting to receive the Colours, are Lts White and Church.

The Colour party of the 4th Battalion with the newly presented Colours, 3 August 1927. From left to right: CQMS Wilkins; Lt White (King's Colour); CSM Smith; Lt Church (Regimental Colour); CQMS Waters. These Colours were carried for forty years until the battalion became part of the newly formed Wessex Regiment. An estimated 3,000 people attended the laying-up service in Salisbury Cathedral on 12 March 1967, filling every seat and standing in the side aisles. The congregation included a number of old soldiers who had been at the 1927 presentation.

1937: the 4th Battalion party that represented the regiment at the Coronation parade in London with the King's Colour. Of the three officers and twenty-eight other ranks in the party, one officer and two other ranks marched in the procession while the other members lined the streets near Marble Arch. The remainder of the battalion were involved in local parades throughout Wiltshire.

Mustapha Barracks, Alexandria, 22 December 1930. Whenever operations allowed, the 1st Battalion commemorated the Battle of Ferozeshah each year on a date as near 21 December as possible. At Ferozeshah (1845) heavy casualties among the officers meant that many companies ended up being commanded by sergeants. The ceremony recalled that occasion with the Colours being entrusted to the sergeants for safekeeping for the day, before being returned to the officers at midnight. Here we see the sergeants' Colour party on the right, carrying the Colours after handover from the officers.

On 13 January 1939 the Viceroy of India, the Marquess of Linlithgow, presented new Colours to the 1st Battalion in Bangalore. From left to right, standing: ADC to Viceroy; Capt. Slee; Lt Wort (King's Colour); Lt Lord Seymore; Lt Stevenson; Lt Cunninghame (Regimental Colour); Lt (QM) Newton, MM; 2nd/Lt Ferro. Front row: Capt. Ashley; Maj. Beaven; Lt Hunter; Col. Segreave; The Viceroy; Maj Ponsford, MC; Maj. Oldfield; Maj. Ludford; Capt. Wood. Lt Hunter became the Colonel of the Duke of Edinburgh's Royal Regiment (Berkshire and Wiltshire) in 1969.

Above: The 1st Battalion commemorate the battle of Ferozeshah, Fort St George, Madras, India, 1940. The commanding officer, Lt–Col. Kellett, DSO, MC (mounted) faces the parade. The Colours are ceremoniously handed over to Sergeants Hollingsworth and Morley. Prior to the handover, the commanding officer's address to the parade included the following: 'Safeguard and honour these Colours as your Officers have ever done and let the fact that our Colours are entrusted to your keeping be not only a reminder of past services but also a visible expression of the confidence and trust which today your Officers justly place in you.'

Below: The Regimental Depot at Devizes was not used for infantry training during the Second World War. Instead, all recruits went to Hyderabad Barracks, Colchester. Here we see the Wiltshire contingent commemorating the Battle of Ferozeshah in a scaled down parade. These Colours belong to either the 2nd or 4th Battalion. The soldiers, all in battle dress, present arms as the Colours are brought to the two Colour Sergeants (wearing the white Colour belts). At this time the Colchester barracks were under the command of Lt–Col. Shepherd, OBE, MC, of the Wiltshire Regiment.

Right: The railway station, Corsham, Wiltshire, September 1947. The cased Colours of the 1st Battalion are carried by Lts Etherington and Fairclough, following the return from India. The battalion was stationed in various camps around Corsham while its numbers returned to post-war levels, reducing from 900 strong to a small nucleus as hundreds of men went back to civilian life and none came to replace them. On 3 December 1947 the battalion took part in the ceremony bestowing the Freedom of Salisbury on the Regiment. It later went to Krefeld, Germany, to join the 2nd Battalion, with which it subsequently amalgamated due to the post-war reductions of Infantry Battalions.

Below: On 1 January 1949, the 1st and 2nd Battalions amalgamated at Krefeld in West Germany. The photograph shows the Colours of both battalions being marched back to the Officers' Mess after the parade. The 1st Battalion thereafter kept both sets of Colours until they were laid up just prior to the amalgamation with the Royal Berkshire Regiment in 1959.

Le Marchant Barracks, Devizes, 18 April 1950. Lt F.J. Stone hands over the 1st Battalion King's Colour to Drum-Major Pegg outside the Officers' Mess following the arrival of the 1st Battalion in Wiltshire. Left: presenting arms are Sgts Brimson; Worman; Warner and Hudd. Standing between the Colours is CSM Baldry. The Colours remained here until the regiment embarked for the Far East in August 1950.

Southampton Docks, 1 August 1950. The Colour party of the 1st Battalion embark on HMT *Empire Trooper* bound for Malaya. Carrying the cased Colours are, from left to right: 2nd/Lt D.A. Parks; 2nd/Lt R. Barnes; 2nd/Lt Money-Kyrle. While on voyage, the ship received a message diverting the battalion to Hong Kong, to replace the brigade that had been sent to South Korea following the invasion by the North.

The 1st Battalion march through Hong Kong during one of the many ceremonial parades that took place in 1950–52. Despite providing drafts for Korea and patrolling the border with China, the battalion maintained a very high level of parade efficiency. Here we see the Queen's Colour (left) and the Regimental Colour with escort.

The 1st Battalion march with their Colours during the Queen's Birthday Parade in Cyprus, 1958. This was during the EOKA campaign in which the battalion was heavily involved. There were a large number of National Servicemen in the battalion at this time but regimental standards were high as is clear from the smart appearance of these troops. On this occasion the Colour party has added protection in the form of a soldier with his loaded SMG at 'the ready' in case of a terrorist attack. The sergeant at the front is Jack Barrow. He later became the fourth Regimental sergeant major of the Duke of Edinburgh's Royal Regiment.

The Colours, drums and regimental silver of the 1st Battalion on the Isle of Wight, 1959. This was the last official regimental function before amalgamation with the Royal Berkshire Regiment to form the Duke of Edinburgh's Royal Regiment (Berkshire and Wiltshire) which took place at Albany Barracks, Isle of Wight, on 9 June 1959. The Battle Honours earned by the Wiltshire Regiment were carried over to the new regiment.

The Colours of the 1st and 2nd Battalions are carried into Salisbury Cathedral to be laid up, prior to the amalgamation, 4 May 1959. From left to right: Lt Canning (Queen's Colour); CSM Young; Lt Rendle (Regimental Colour). They are followed by the Colours of the 2nd Battalion carried by 2nd/Lt Larkman and Lt Shears. These soldiers are wearing the Wessex Brigade cap badge, regimental cap badges having been discontinued the previous year.

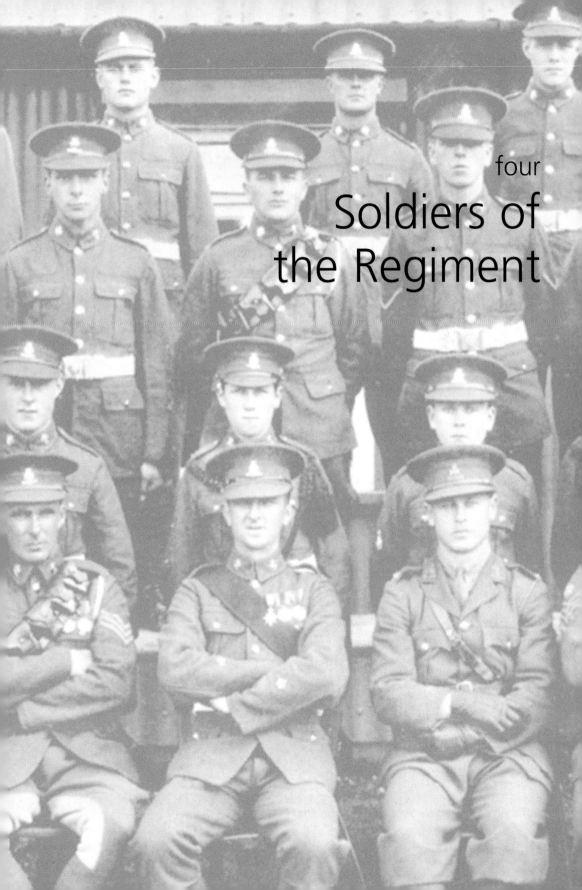

four

Soldiers of the Regiment

Above left: Reginald Frederick Johnson Hayward, VC, was born in East Griqualand, South Africa, on 17 June 1891. He played for Natal against the touring English rugby teams before coming to England in 1912. Entering the Royal College of Veterinary Surgeons, he also played rugby for Rosslyn Park and Middlesex. He joined up when war broke out in 1914 and was commissioned as a 2nd/Lt in the 6th Battalion. He transferred to the 1st Battalion in 1915 and remained with them until 1919, being wounded, but remaining on duty, at Messines. He briefly commanded the battalion at the end of 1917. He won his Victoria Cross in 1918, the citation reads:

> For most conspicuous bravery in action. This officer while in command of a company displayed almost superhuman powers of endurance and consistent courage of the rarest nature. In spite of the fact that he was buried, wounded in the head and rendered deaf on the first day of operations and had his arm shattered two days late he refused to leave his men (even though he received a third serious injury to his head) until he collapsed from sheer physical exhaustion. Throughout the whole of this period the enemies were attacking his company front without cessation, but Capt Hayward continued to move across the open ground from one trench to another with absolute disregard of his own personal safety, concentrating entirely on reorganising his defence and encouraging his men. It was almost entirely due to the magnificent example of ceaseless energy of this officer that many most determined attacks upon his portion of the trench system failed entirely.

He carried the 1st Battalion's King's Colour at the victory parade in London and Paris in 1919. Captain Hayward stayed on as a regular officer in the Wiltshires after the First World War, later becoming Adjutant of the 3rd Wiltshires. He retired in 1935. During the Second World War he served with the Royal Army Service Corps, and from 1945–47 commanded Prisoner of War camps. He died in London in 1970.

Above right: Pte Gadden, an 'Old Contemptible' of 'A' Company, 1st Battalion, in trench 'J3' at Kemmel, Belgium, December 1914. This photo gives a clear picture of the conditions that infantry soldiers endured during the early stages of the war. The trench systems had yet to develop into something more substantial and he is equipped with only a greatcoat to keep out the inclement weather. Pte Gadden survived the war.

Above left: CSM Sidney Pearce, Military Cross, Distinguished Conduct Medal, Military Medal and Bar, Medaille Militaire 1st Battalion. He was one of the most highly decorated soldiers of the Wiltshire Regiment in the First World War. He enlisted in the Wiltshire Regiment in 1905 and went to France in 1914, remaining in the battalion throughout the war. His citation for the Military Cross reads:

> This Warrant Officer showed the greatest courage and initiative in an attack on a village, when his company was heavily fired on by machine guns. He went forward, captured an officer, and forced him to reveal the positions of four enemy machine guns. He then worked round to the rear of the guns and succeeded in putting them all out of action. Throughout the operations he set a splendid example.

His DCM citation reads:

> For conspicuous gallantry and devotion to duty throughout continuous fighting. He was invaluable to the regiment in controlling and encouraging the men and materially assisted in holding many important positions. In a counter attack he showed great courage in advancing ahead of the attacking troops with a Lewis gun and killed no less than 18 of the enemy. His fine example inspired all ranks.

He was wounded once and was discharged in 1919 after thirteen years' service. Re-enlisting in 1941 into the Queen's Regiment, he served in its 11th and 30th Battalions for the next three years before being discharged in 1944. He died at Guildford in 1967. His medals are on display in the Regimental Museum, Salisbury.

Above right: Lt Geoffrey Killigrew Wait, MC, 1st Battalion, Bouzincourt, 1916 (with his arm in a sling). He won his Military Cross in a daring raid east of Ploegsteert Wood in 1917. He was wounded again on 13 August 1918. Remaining in the regiment after the war, he was still serving in 1938. During the Second World War he was attached to the Royal Air Force. He was killed in an air crash on the Isle of Man on 23 August 1942 and is buried at Andreas (St Andrew) churchyard, Isle of Man.

Capt. Charles Alfred Brooks, Wiltshire Regiment and Royal Flying Corps. He was born in Turleigh in Wiltshire in 1888, and before coming of age spent four years at sea as a merchant seaman. On the outbreak of war in 1914, he was granted a special reserve commission in the Wiltshire Regiment. He joined the 2nd Battalion, fighting at Neuve Chapelle in March 1915, receiving a gunshot wound to his left leg. While convalescing, he decided to join the Royal Flying Corps, and in September 1915 received his Royal Aero Club certificate, No.1947. He returned to France where on 1 March 1916 he was again wounded when his aircraft crashed. After a posting to Egypt where he joined the flying school at Aboukir as a flying instructor, he went to No.67 (Australian) Squadron. On 8 July 1917, while on patrol in a Matinsyde aeroplane, he was attacked by two German Scout aircraft near Gaza. Brooks spun away to avoid the attack, and as he did so the wings of his aircraft were seen to fold up and the tail to fall off. The German aviator Felmy sent a letter to the squadron to say that Capt. Brooks had been buried with full Military Honours. His grave was never found and he is commemorated on the Jerusalem Memorial to the missing.

Capt. Cary Barnard (left) and officers of 'C' Company, 1st Battalion, in Ridor Wood, near Dickebushe, Belgium, 1914. He joined the regiment in 1900 after service with Lumsden's Horse in the Boer War. Following service in India with the 1st Battalion, he joined the West Africa Regiment for three years. He rejoined the 1st Battalion in France on 22 October 1914, and won the first of two Distinguished Service Orders at Hooge the next month, when he led a bayonet charge that regained some trenches. He later commanded the 1st Battalion for a short period, followed by command of the 68th Brigade. For his services in the war he was awarded the DSO and Bar, the CMG, was Mentioned in Dispatches seven times and received the Italian Croix de Guerre and order of St Maurice and St Lazarus. He later became the base commander in Taranto, Italy, returning to command the 1st Battalion after the end of the war. He then transferred to the Tank Corps and retired in 1927. He died in Tanganyika in 1932, aged fifty-six.

Above left: Capt. Charles Notley, 4th Battalion, seen here wearing a goatskin jacket that provided some protection from the adverse winter conditions but at the same time attracted visitors such as lice and fleas! Born in Salisbury, he became Assistant City Surveyor in 1906. Prior to the First World War he served for fourteen years with the 1st Wiltshire Volunteer Battalion (later the 4th Battalion). On the outbreak of war he mobilised with the 4th Battalion and then went to India with the 1st/4th, remaining with it for approximately a year, by which time he had been promoted to sergeant. He returned to England, was commissioned and then posted to the 2nd/5th North Staffordshire Regiment on the Western Front. At the end of the war, he joined the 1st Battalion Wiltshires, who were re-forming in Dublin. In 1919 he resigned his commission and became chief officer of Salisbury Volunteer Fire Brigade. He died in 1954, aged seventy-two.

Above right: Major T.E. (QM) Brewer, MBE. Known as 'Dick', he enlisted into the regiment on 17 August 1905. Initially posted to the band of the 2nd Battalion, who were at that time stationed at Bordon, he later spent time at Pembroke Dock, Dublin, Gosport and Gibraltar. He went to France in 1914. Remaining with the 2nd Battalion throughout the war as a platoon sergeant, he fought with it in all its engagements, resisting all attempts to send him back to England in a training capacity. In 1919 he went with the battalion's contingent to Archangel as part of the North Russian Relief Force. After this posting he rejoined the 2nd Battalion in Hong Kong, followed by Bangalore and Kamptee. In 1926 he was appointed RSM of the 1st Battalion (at that time stationed in Plymouth), followed by the battalion's move to Alexandria where he was later awarded an MBE for outstanding service. He was commissioned in 1933, rejoining the 2nd Battalion in Plymouth and then remaining with them at Aldershot and in Palestine. During the Second World War he was the Quartermaster of 15 Infantry Training Centre, retiring after the war with forty-four years of service. He died in 1956.

Above left: Pte Edward Sturgess. He joined the 2nd Battalion in October 1914, taking part in the battles of Ypres, Langemarck, Neuve Chapelle, Aubers, Festubert, Montauban, Guillemont, Trones Wood, Hindenburg Line, Pilkem Ridge, Messines, and St Quentin. He was with the battalion at L'Epine de Dallon on 21 March 1918, when it was completely overwhelmed after inflicting significant casualties on the advancing German Army. The battalion lost twenty-two officers and over 600 other ranks either killed, wounded or taken prisoner, with very few escaping. Pte Sturgess was one of those captured. He later remembered:

> We were now ready for any attack which we thought really would never come off but we spotted some black objects running about so we let fly with all we had which was very effective on the foe but the misfortune now must come when at a quarter to twelve the Germans made an attack but was forced back but they came again and out numbered us at 3.30 p.m. We were surrounded and captured but not before we had spent all our ammunition and destroyed our guns.

Pte Sturgess was a lucky man. At the 1st Battle of Ypres he was hit in the head, but his cap badge deflected the bullet (see inset). At the end of the war he returned to England, and after two months' leave he resumed his pre-war occupation as a tram driver for Swindon Corporation. He married in 1920 and died in 1960 at the age of sixty-seven.

Above right: Sholto Stewart Ogilvie was born in 1884. He was a barrister who served in the Honourable Artillery Company, transferring to the 1st Battalion Wiltshires as a corporal shortly after the First Battle of Ypres in Oct 1914. Commissioned in early 1915, he had become a captain by the time of the Battle of Loos in September that year. In July 1916 he took over temporary command of the 1st Battalion when Lt-Col. W.S. Brown was killed in the Somme offensive. The next month he was slightly wounded in the leg during the defeat of the Prussian Guard at Thiepval, but remained on duty. On 3 September that year he was again wounded in the leg during an unsuccessful attack near Thiepval. He was again temporarily in command in early 1917 before being promoted to Lt-Col. In June. He commanded the 1st Battalion from June 1917 to April 1918 with great courage and skill and had two short spells as Acting Brigade Commander. After the second of these, in February 1918 he returned to the battalion in time to command it at the Battle of Bapaume, during which he won his third DSO. The Germans attacked again on 10 April at the Battle of the Lys and the 1st Battalion was once again decimated. He was captured on 12 April 1918. While in captivity, he made use of his legal knowledge defending any PoW who was in trouble with the prison authorities. He was repatriated on 4 December 1918 and died in 1961.

Above left: On 23 October 1918, the 1st Battalion took part in a night attack on Vendegies and Ovillers. The enemy artillery opened up on the battalion as it was forming up on the start line; nevertheless, it advanced in good order but suffered further casualties through flanking machine gun fire. The battalion gained its objective, sustaining 150 casualties with twenty-five killed. Of those who died, twenty were buried nearby at Poix-du-Nord, with a grave marker carved and erected by Pioneer Sgt Gunther. This marked the graves of 2nd/Lts Palmer, Cooper; CSM Bray, DCM; Cpl Bowden; L/Cpls Lowe, Ervane; Ptes Pitman, Mason, Trent, Sawyer, Connor, Elson, North, Terry, Dyball, Martin, Mace, Sharples, Weaver, and Richardson. Most of these men were later re-interred by the Imperial War Graves Commission in Ovillers Military Cemetery. Fighting ended nineteen days later.

Above right: Col. Walter Leslie Rocke. He was born in 1862 and commissioned into the Wiltshire Regiment in 1882. He retired in 1905 but was recalled in 1914 to form and command the 7th (Service) Battalion. His first order on taking over the battalion was to instruct all his officers to send home for their dinner jackets to wear in their 'Hotel' Mess at Marlborough in lieu of mess kit. The battalion was made up of drafts from Wiltshire, South Wales (mostly coalminers from Hirwain), London, Wolverton (LNW Railway Works), Birmingham and Yorkshire. An officer of the battalion later remembered:

> The Wolverton draft were intended for the Oxford and Bucks Lt-Col. Rocke, who had a very keen eye for large and strong men, saw the draft being marched in. He asked them who they were and received the reply that they had orders to go to the Oxs and Bucks. He immediately ordered them to march to his camp. 'But Sir....,' 'Do as I b----y well tell you'. They did and they stayed.

He trained the battalion hard and men were soon completing thirty-mile marches in a day with full packs. He commanded the battalion for nearly three years, in France and Salonika. Known to the troops as 'Old Bonny', he always wore his best London wash-leather gloves. He died in 1932.

Above left: Capt. Herbert 'Bert' Waylen, MC, was born on 31 October 1873, one of three sons of QMS William Waylen who served in the 62nd Foot and Wiltshire Regiment for over thirty years. All three sons enlisted in the regiment. Capt. Waylen served with 3rd Wiltshires in St Helena during the Boer War and was commissioned into the Wiltshire Regiment on 5 September 1914. Between 22 September and 13 November 1915 he served in France and Belgium, then went to Greek Macedonia until 6 July 1917. He was wounded once and was awarded the Military Cross and twice Mentioned in Dispatches. By the time he retired in 1920, he had risen to the rank of major.

Above right: Sgt Frederick Mundy, DCM. He was a pre-war Territorial soldier who had served in the 4th Battalion Hampshire Regiment. Before the war he was a school teacher in Bradford-on-Avon. On the outbreak of war he joined the 1st/4th Battalion Wiltshire Regiment which went to India to relieve a regular regiment for service on the Western Front. He remained there until 1917 when he moved to Egypt with his battalion, which went into action at Gaza for the first time on 6 November 1917. Later at El Kustineh he won the DCM, the citation reading, 'For conspicuous gallantry and devotion to duty. He with the assistance of one other NCO (Sgt Couldrey) captured two officers, forty other ranks and two machine guns. These men completed this bold and gallant deed entirely unassisted by other troops.' He was discharged in 1919, returning to the teaching profession in Bradford-on-Avon. Soldiering clearly appealed to him and in 1920 he rejoined the Territorials, serving long enough to qualify for the Territorial Efficiency Medal. He was later appointed headmaster at Rushall School, and retired in 1951. He died in 1972. During his service he maintained a vivid record of his experiences which is still used by Regimental historians.

Above left: Sgt Arthur George Howes, 1st/4th Battalion, in the trenches near Gaza, 1917. He was the platoon sergeant for Lt Tucker, who took this photograph. Sgt Howes was born in Laverstock, Wiltshire, and enlisted at Salisbury. This photograph was taken at 4 p.m. on 8 November 1917; he was Killed in Action at 11 p.m. the same day. He is buried in the Dier El Belah War Cemetery.

Above right: Capt. Christopher Ken Merewether, 1st/4th Battalion. He came from North Bradley, Wiltshire, and was the son of the Rev. Canon Merewether from Salisbury. Before the war he studied at Oriel College, Oxford where he took honours in modern history. On leaving the university, he was selected by the directors of the White Star Line of Liverpool for training as an assistant manager. He is seen here in Egypt prior to going to Palestine. He was a company commander and was seriously wounded during the battalion's attack at El Mesmiyeh on 13 November 1917, receiving a gunshot wound that paralysed him. Evacuated back to Port Said, he died of his wounds there on 20 December and was buried in the Port Said War Memorial Cemetery. He was very highly regarded by his men, being described by one of his sergeants, Sgt Mundy, who won a DCM in the same action, as 'Our gallant Captain'. During this battle the battalion lost ten other ranks killed, and three officers and eighty-eight other ranks wounded.

Above: 'Sons of the Regiment' at Lucknow Barracks, Tidworth, *c.*1926. These were soldiers serving with the 1st Battalion whose fathers and grandfathers had also served in the regiment. From left to right, back row: Boy Roberts; Ptes Langley, Perry, Heathorne, Cook, Nutland. Second row: Ptes Dale, Coster, Harding; L/Cpl Harries; Ptes Stone, Lovegrove, Titchner. Third row: Boy Dunkley; Ptes Best, Boys, McCarracher, Regan, Barnfield, Worsdell, Brown. Front row: L/Cpl Griffiths; Sgt Marcks; CSM Burrows; 2nd/Lt Day; CQMS Burrows; Band Sgt Bartholomew; Cpl Hart. 2nd/Lt Day's forebears had served in the 99th Foot as far back as 1860 during the China War. He served with the 1st Battalion until 1931, joining the Iraq Levies taking part in the campaign against Sheik Ahmed of Barzan, followed by service with the 2nd Battalion in Palestine. He went to France on the outbreak of war, remaining with the 2nd Battalion throughout the retreat to Dunkirk. In Burma he served as a staff officer under General Alexander. He became the Second in Command of the 2nd Battalion at Hanover and Krefeld 1947/48, and retired in 1951 as a Lieutenant Colonel.

Above left: Lt-Col. Percy Stewart Rowan, DSO. Born in 1882 he joined the Wiltshires from the Militia in 1901. He was adjutant of the 1st Battalion from 1911 to 1915, fighting with it in France, where he was twice wounded. On the second occasion at Neuve Chapelle he was hit by three bullets when leading an attack. Afterwards, he remained in France on the staff until 1918. In addition to his DSO he was Mentioned in Dispatches four times. Following staff appointments in Ireland, Turkey and Malta, he became second in command of the 2nd Battalion in 1925. He was a good horseman, cricketer and boxer. He took command of the 1st Battalion in Egypt, and was killed in an air crash at Ismalia in October 1931. He was buried at Alexandria.

Above right: Lt Frank Eyres, DCM, MM, 4th Battalion. He was born in Northleigh Terrace, Wilton, in 1919 and on leaving school became a gardener at Wilton House, Wiltshire. On the outbreak of war he joined his local Territorial unit, the 4th Battalion. He landed in Europe with the battalion on 19 June 1944 and took part in all its actions. Prominent in the assault on the Chateau de Maltot, he was awarded a Military Medal for rescuing and tending the wounded. Later, during the operations around Elst, Holland, on 4 October 1944, when the other platoons were pinned down by enemy fire he took 18 Platoon, 'D' Company (which consisted of only ten of the original forty men) forward to mop up the enemy. This they did, in the process capturing ninety-eight prisoners. He himself took several machine-gun posts. For this action he was awarded the Distinguished Conduct Medal and a commission in the field. A few days after this he was wounded by shrapnel and lost one eye. He was later presented with his DCM by the King at Buckingham Palace. He died in 2002.

Opposite below: Lts B.A. Coad (left) and O.F. Newton-Dunn, two subalterns of the Wiltshire Regiment. They are seen here on a tandem in 1935, during a bet in which they claimed they would cycle from Plymouth (where they were stationed with the 2nd Battalion in Crownhill Barracks) to London in twenty-four hours. They won the bet, completing the ride in seventeen hours, thirty-five minutes. Lt Coad went on to have a long and illustrious career. He was a fine all-round games player, both for the regiment and the county of Wiltshire. He served at all levels within the regiment, winning a DSO and Bar in the Second World War. After the war he commanded the 27th Brigade in the Korean War and then the 2nd Division in Germany. He became the last colonel of the Wiltshire Regiment in 1954, and on its amalgamation with the Royal Berkshire Regiment in 1959, became the first colonel of the Duke of Edinburgh's Royal Regiment. He died in 1981 and was buried in Tidworth Military Cemetery.

Above left: Pte Geoff Young, 4th Battalion. He was born in 1921, spending his formative years in Shrewton, Wiltshire. In 1939 he joined his county Territorial Battalion. In June 1944 he landed at Normandy, going into action at St Manvieu on 26 June 1944. He fought with the 4th Battalion at Hill 112, Maltot, Mont Pincon, and at the crossing of the river Seine. After the Seine action, the battalion took part in Operation Market Garden. At one point Young was captured, but after nearly being killed by German 'friendly fire', his fortunes were reversed and his captors became his prisoners. The battalion then went to the Reichswald Forest where constant patrolling became the priority. He remained with the battalion throughout, ending up in a camp next to Belsen. Pte Young received the Dutch Bronze Cross, he was Mentioned in Dispatches and received the Commander-in-Chief's Certificate for outstanding service. He was also recommended for the Military Medal (twice) and the American Distinguished Service Cross – the latter for his single-handed assistance to an American parachute company of the 101st Airborne Division during Operation Market Garden. He is pictured here in Hengelo, Holland, in 1945. The 43rd Wessex Division shoulder flash, The Wyvern is visible on his right shoulder.

Above right: Sgt 'Alex' Alexander, 4th Battalion. He joined the battalion in May 1939, attending his first camp in July the same year. Mobilised on the outbreak of the Second World War, his first billet was the guard room at Upavon, a building he himself had helped construct while working for W.E. Chivers & Sons. He joined the carrier platoon, attending numerous courses and rising through the ranks to Corporal. His platoon's first casualty was a L/Cpl, killed by German shellfire at Deal in Kent. He landed at Normandy on D Day + 10 and was later wounded on the advance to Hill 112, when the carrier he was in was blown up by a land mine. He arrived back with the battalion in time for the abortive attempt to reach the airborne troops at Arnhem, but was later wounded for a second time at Geilenkirchen by a long-range German shell. After hospital treatment, he rejoined the battalion for the Bremen operation. Following a period of leave, he again rejoined the battalion, now involved with the administration and cleaning-up of the Belsen concentration camp. Here his platoon was involved with the burning of the camp buildings in order to prevent the spread of disease. He was demobbed at the end of the war but rejoined the battalion when it was re-formed a few years later.

Sgt Maurice Rogers, VC, MM. Born in Bristol, his family came from the Marlborough area. He enlisted in the Army at the age of fourteen as a boy soldier and was posted to the 2nd Battalion, joining his brother who was already in the corps of drums. He was a prominent member of the battalion athletic team, which won the Northern Command Athletic Championships in 1939. He was promoted to the rank of Lance Corporal in the same year. On the outbreak of the Second World War he went with the 2nd Battalion to France, surviving the evacuation from the beaches of Dunkirk. In 1941 he was promoted to sergeant, becoming the Carrier platoon sergeant. He remained with the 2nd Battalion throughout, and in Sicily in August 1943, he won his Military Medal at Farm Landolina. On 3 September 1943, he was part of the invasion force that landed in Italy.

Sgt Rogers attacks a machine-gun position held by the 4th German Parachute Division at Ardea, 3 June 1944. This was a significant battle for the battalion and Sgt Rogers' action broke the deadlock. Although he was shot and killed at point-blank range, his actions encouraged his platoon to clear the remainder of the trenches. The final paragraph of Sgt Rogers' VC citation reads, 'This N.C.O.'s undaunted determination, fearless devotion to duty and superb courage carried his platoon on to their objective in face of a determined enemy in a strongly defended position. The great gallantry and heroic self-sacrifice of Sergeant Rogers were in the highest traditions of the British Army.' The painting shown above was commissioned by the warrant officers' and Sergeants' Mess of the 1st Battalion Duke of Edinburgh's Royal Regiment.

Major Derek Robbins, 4th Battalion, receives the award of the Military Cross from Field Marshall Montgomery, 24 April 1945. He was commissioned into the Wiltshire Regiment in August 1938. After a short spell with the 1st Battalion in India, he returned home in 1941 to the 5th Battalion, then later transferred to the 4th. He fought throughout the campaign in North-West Europe with this battalion. He was wounded three times and was awarded the Military Cross after the action on 'The Island' near Nijmegen. After attending post-war staff college, he served with the 1st Battalion in Hong Kong, Cyprus and the UK. In 1960 he commanded the 4th Battalion. He became a very strong supporter of the Old Comrades Association and the Regimental Museum.

Lt-Col. N.C.E. Kenrick, DSO, born in 1905, joined the 1st Battalion in 1925, serving with it until 1939. On the outbreak of the Second World War, he became a Staff Capt.ain in India. In 1940 he returned to England, joining the 2nd Battalion as it re-formed after Dunkirk. He then became the Second in Command of the 7th Battalion. Assuming command of the 5th Battalion in 1942, he led it to Normandy in 1944. During this time he was wounded but resumed command, taking the battalion to the borders of Germany. Early in 1945, he was acting brigade commander in the advance to the Rhine, and was awarded a DSO after the capture of Cleve. He commanded the 1st Battalion from 1946 to 1948, much of the time spent on internal security duty in Calcutta, Amritsar and Lahore. After a spell with the Military Mission in Greece in 1948, he returned to command the 2nd Battalion in Germany, and to amalgamate them with the 1st Battalion. He represented the regiment in five different sports, and Combined Services Malaya at rugby and hockey. He retired in 1958 as the Garrison Commander of Tidworth and Bulford. After retirement, he wrote the regimental history. He died in 1976.

Sgt 'Ozzie' Osbourne, 1st Battalion, Hanover, *c.*1947. Sgt Osbourne joined the 2nd Battalion near Etna in Sicily as a bren gun carrier driver with the mortar platoon after service in North Africa with the Queen's Regiment. He stayed with the battalion for the rest of the war, fighting with it at the crossing of the river Garigliano, Anzio, the road to Rome and Germany. He remained in the Army after the war and was a regular rider for the British Army of the Rhine speedway team, competing on a regular basis against all-comers. Here he is leading the way at the Hanovermag stadium. He retired from the Army in 1948 and was then a milkman for some years.

Pte Ken Barrington, 1st Battalion. Son of a regular soldier in the Royal Berkshire Regiment, Ken was born in Brock Barracks, Reading. He was a National Serviceman who served in the Wiltshire Regiment in Germany and Hong Kong. He was a cricketer of note and made his debut for Surrey Colts in 1947. On joining the 1st Battalion, he was immediately placed in both the battalion and Army teams. Lt-Col. Kenrick wrote that the battalion 'was much strengthened by the arrival of a national service soldier called Barrington, who is a Surrey colt and a very promising all-round cricketer, leg break bowling being his particular forte'. Barrington later remembered with amusement that when picked to play for the Army, 'I found myself the only squaddie in a team of officers, when the team arrived at Ostend by boat, four staff cars took the Officers to the game, whereas I had to travel by lorry'. After leaving the Army, he had an excellent career as batsman in the English Test Cricket team. This unfortunately came to a close in 1969, when he suffered a heart attack. He died in 1981.

Sgt Arthur John Minty (right) was born in the Barracks at Devizes in 1913, and enlisted into the 4th (TA) Battalion in 1931. Joining the regular Army in 1933, he went to India with the 1st Battalion in 1936. After the outbreak of the Second World War, he was posted back to England where he joined the 5th Battalion. He went to France with this battalion and was wounded during its heroic crossing of the river Seine. After the war he held a number of posts but he is remembered for his time as a recruit instructor at Devizes. His father also served in the regiment, dying in service in Shanghai in 1929 while serving in the 2nd Battalion, and his great-grandfather was the canteen sergeant in the Regiment as far back as 1870. His youngest son, Norman, followed his footsteps into the amalgamated regiment, the Duke of Edinburgh's Royal Regiment, serving for many years and retiring as a Lt-Col. CSM Shord (left), had a brother who also served in the regiment. Both had just received their Long Service and Good Conduct Medals from the Duke of Edinburgh.

Col. Jack Houghton-Brown, DSO, TD, seen here raising a glass in 1956 on his retirement as Hon. Col. of the 4th Battalion. Born in 1906, he joined the 4th Battalion as a Territorial soldier on leaving school, later taking up command of the Warminster Platoon. Following the outbreak of the Second World War, he joined the 1st Battalion in the Far East, taking over command on the eve of active service in the Arakan. He was severely wounded at Hill 551. After the war he returned to farming, but later joined the Territorials when they were reformed. His son joined the regiment as a National Service Officer, serving in Cyprus with the 1st Battalion. Col. Houghton-Brown died in 1983.

Brig. George Wort, CBE, seen here with a photograph of the Carrickfergus cup. He was commissioned into the Wiltshire Regiment in 1932, and was later seconded to the Malay Regiment. Captured by the Japanese in 1943, he spent time in Changi Jail where his left arm was amputated by Japanese doctors. He was released in 1945 and later commanded the 4th (TA) Battalion for three years. Subsequently, he commanded the 109 Ulster Brigade, before retiring in 1961. He joined Wiltshire County Council, becoming an alderman in 1970, and deputy lieutenant of Wiltshire in 1968. Brig. Wort died in 1984. His son joined the Duke of Edinburgh's Royal Regiment.

The officers at the Regimental Depot, Le Marchant Barracks, Devizes, 1953-54. From left to right, back row: Lt A.E. Carter (Training Subaltern); Maj. (Rtd) G.W. Richardson (Admin Officer); Lt J.M. Hartland (Training Subaltern); Lt (QM) J. Harrowing. From left to right, front row: Maj. F.R.E. Turner (OC Training Company); Maj. The Duke of Somerset (Commanding Officer); Capt. T.A. Gibson (Adjutant). These officers were responsible for ensuring that recruits reached the required standard before posting to the battalion. Lt Carter was the only officer from the regiment to serve in both Malaya and Korea. Capt. Gibson became the fifth commanding officer of the 1st Battalion Duke of Edinburgh's Royal Regiment in 1967.

Above left: Sgt Don Briggs, 1st Battalion. He initially joined the Gloucestershire Regiment, but after training remained at the depot as an instructor. Later transferring to the 2nd Battalion Wiltshire Regiment in Krefeld, Germany, he took part in the amalgamation parade. In 1950, the regiment was due to be deployed to Malaya. Sgt Briggs formed part of the advance party, taking part in training and operations with the Suffolk Regiment. He is pictured here with a No.5 Rifle which was used for jungle operations. This training was cut short when the regiment was diverted to Hong Kong. He served there for three years, followed by postings to Warminster as part of the Army demonstration battalion, then three years active service in Cyprus during the EOKA campaign. Remaining in the regiment after the amalgamation with the Royal Berkshires, he served in the new Duke of Edinburgh's Royal Regiment in Tidworth, Nassau, and Malta. He was posted to the 4th Territorial Battalion at Devizes, and later became the RQMS for the 2nd Division in Germany. After retirement, he helped to form the Bristol branch of the Regimental Association, and served on the executive committee.

Above right: Lt-Col. G.F. Woolnough, MC. He was the last commanding officer of the 1st Battalion and the first for the 1st Battalion, The Duke of Edinburgh's Royal Regiment (Berkshire and Wiltshire), into which he was quick to instil the traditions and history of both predecessor regiments. He was commissioned into the 2nd Battalion in 1935, having passed out third in the order of merit from Sandhurst. He was the adjutant of the 2nd Battalion on the outbreak of the Second World War and went with it to France and Belgium, subsequently being Mentioned in Dispatches. After the evacuation through Dunkirk, he had a short period with both staff and the 4th Battalion before rejoining the 2nd Battalion in 1941. As a Company Commander, he remained with the 2nd until 1945, serving in Madagascar, India, the Middle East, Sicily, Italy (where he was awarded the Military Cross) and finally Germany during the final stages of the war. After the war he held staff appointments in Germany, Burma and Malaya. He later became a Lt-Col. at the Iraqi Army Staff College. In addition to being a fine all-round sportsman, he was an accomplished amateur artist. He is seen here wearing the Wessex Brigade cap badge, worn from 1958–68, together with the collar badges of the Duke of Edinburgh's Royal Regiment.

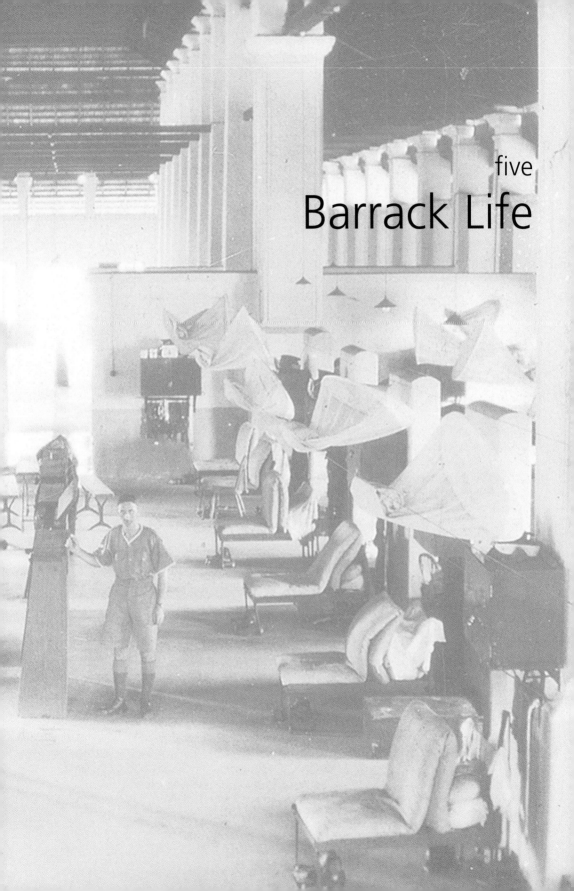

five
Barrack Life

Built 1898. The depot of the Wilts (Duke of Edinburgh's Regiment) The present Great War has caused great activity here during four weeks in Aug. and Sept., 1914, over 5,000 men were enlisted and over 3,000 Reservists were called up.

Devizes Barracks.

The keep and main gate at Le Marchant Barracks, Devizes, c.1915. This was the regimental depot, and had been since 1878 when the 62nd Foot (1st Battalion) and the 99th Foot (2nd Battalion) were grouped together under the Army reforms. On the outbreak of the First World War, the barracks became a hive of activity with around 5,000 soldiers being processed through the system in the first few months. Most of these went to the 1st and 2nd Battalions on the Western Front, which had suffered grievous losses.

The barrack blocks and parade square inside Le Marchant Barracks, Devizes. Initially, it had accommodation for 250 soldiers. It was a self-contained community, with married quarters, a hospital and its own fine cricket ground. Between the wars, most recruits for the regiment did their basic training here. After the Second World War it reverted to its previous function, until 1959. It then became the Depot of The Duke of Edinburgh's Royal Regiment until late 1960, after which all recruit training was undertaken at the Wessex Brigade Depot at Exeter. The 4th (TA) Battalion of the Wiltshire Regiment were the main occupants until 1967, when the 1st Battalion of the newly formed Wessex Regiment took over.

The Officers' Mess, Le Marchant Barracks, Devizes *c.*1916. At this time, the building was being used as a military hospital. This use continued for the duration of the First World War, then it reverted to its previous function.

On the outbreak of the First World War, the number of men joining the Regiment quickly outstripped the facilities available at the Regimental Depot. As a consequence, the Service Battalions (5th, 6th and 7th) had to form up in temporary camps, mainly on Salisbury Plain. Initially these were tented camps, but wooden huts were soon erected. Even so, the conditions were spartan. Here we see a group of 6th Battalion soldiers outside their hut. It is clear from the clothing worn that heating inside the buildings was a luxury.

The Corps of Drums of the 1st/4th Battalion parade at the hill station at Chaubattia, India, c.1916. The battalion remained here from April to November to escape the heat of Delhi. The side drummer second from the right is Drummer Hulbert Heames. He joined the battalion in 1912 and regularly cycled from Swindon to Devizes (twenty-one miles) for practice, with his drum slung on his back. The side drummer on the extreme left is Drummer Albert Fluck from Swindon, the father of Diana Fluck, better known as the British actress Diana Dors. Drummer Fluck later volunteered for service in France, where he was commissioned and seriously wounded.

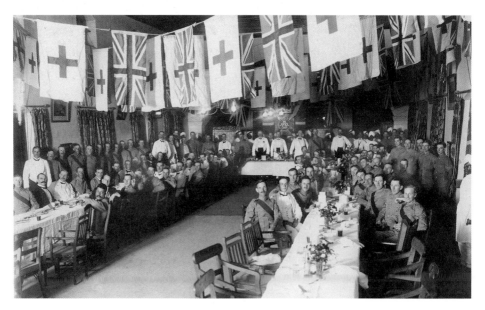

The Sergeants' Mess members and their guests, Christmas 1915, at Poona, India. The 2nd/4th Battalion had sailed for India on 12 December 1914. After carrying out garrison duties in Poona and Kirkee, the battalion moved to Allahabad, where it remained throughout the war, supplying regular drafts of trained soldiers to the 1st/4th. From left top right, top table: Maj. Crosbie, RSM Dopson, Col. Parsons. After leaving the Army, RSM Dopson became the Town Crier for Devizes.

The 5th (Service) Battalion was formed at Assaye Barracks, Tidworth, and later moved to Cowshot. Here we see four officers of the battalion play out a farce entitled *Gentleman Boarders* in the picture house at Cirencester in 1915, where the battalion was preparing for active service. On this occasion, the battalion provided twenty acts arranged by Lt Hill. From left to right: Lt W.F. Jesson (Mr Jasper); Lt F.E. Hill (Sophia Clutterbuck); Lt D.O. Lumley (Grace); Capt. A.C. Belcher (Percy). The proceeds of the performance went to the Belgian relief fund. Capt. Belcher was the Adjutant of the 5th Battalion. He was later Killed in Action on the ridge at Sari Bair, in Gallipoli, on 10 August 1915.

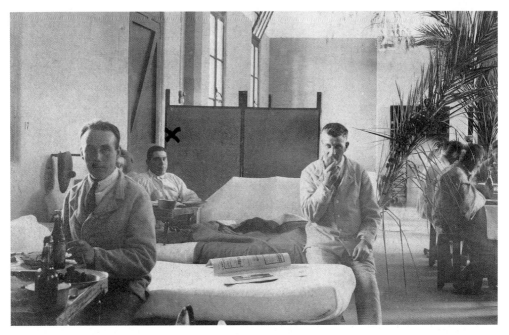

During the First World War, barrack rooms were often converted into extensions of military hospitals. Although run with strict military discipline, the nursing care was usually first-rate, with the prime object of getting patients back to the front line as quickly as possible. Here we see Sgt Couldrey, DCM, 1st/4th Battalion (marked with an X) in a Cairo Military Hospital, Christmas 1917, having been wounded at Enab in Palestine. He later wrote:

> I have often wondered what I must have looked like when I came to hospital. I had one arm in a sling. Both legs bandaged with septic sores (which I got by johnny's barbed wire when we went over at Gaza). My shirt at the back was covered in blood through carrying Harrington when he got wounded. Khaki shorts were filthy dirty and boots and puttees broken. I also had some live stock – real Palestine pals.

As soon as Sgt Couldrey recovered, he returned to active service with the battalion. He survived the war.

Royal Barracks, Dublin, c.1921. The 1st Battalion takes a meal on the parade square. After the First World War, the battalion re-formed at the Barracks, where they remained until 1922. The occasion shown here is not known, but the equipment with piled rifles suggests that it could have been the commemoration parade for Thiepval Day. The table in the centre consists entirely of elderly gentlemen, presumably old soldiers of the regiment in 'mufti'.

'Thiepval Day', Royal Barracks, 1922. A significant number of those who had survived the attack at Thiepval in 1916 were still serving with both battalions. Here we see 1st Battalion veterans being inspected. Present on parade were: Capt. B.K. Wait, MC; Lt A.T. Griffiths, MC, DCM; CSM H.J. Baish; Sgt J. Tovey, MM; Sgt J.J. Sweeney; Sgt E.H. Poolman, MM; L/Cpl R. Goulding; L/Cpl W.C. Bartlett; L/Cpl R. Luckett; Pte C. Cambray, MM; Pte J. Butchart; Pte D. Ingledew; Pte C.E. Smith.

The barrack room of 'D' Company, Christmas 1923. In 1922 the 2nd Battalion moved from Hong Kong to Bangalore, with detachments at Madras. Bangalore was one of the best stations in India, never unduly hot and with the pleasant Nilgiri Hills close by. Here the barrack room has been converted into a dining hall and decorated to give it a homely feel. The tables held enough beer to keep 'D' Company in good spirits!

The funeral of Lt-Col. P.S. Rowan, DSO, Egypt, 1931. Officers and soldiers of the battalion follow the gun carriage carrying the coffin to Alexandria cemetery. Lt-Col. Rowan was the commanding officer of the 1st Battalion, which had arrived at Alexandria the previous year. He was killed in an air crash on 2 October.

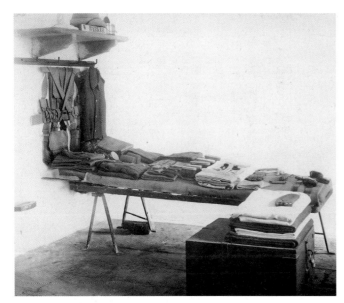

The bed space for Pte W. Barker, 1st Battalion, Egypt, 1930. All his issued equipment and clothing would be laid out in a pre-determined order so that the inspecting officer could see at a glance if anything was missing. It also gave the soldier an understanding of the standards required, which if achieved in barracks would carry over into the field. Soldiers not managing to achieve the standard required would receive extra 'tuition' in the guard room. The only luxuries they were allowed to keep were personal items in the 'soldier's box' at the foot of the bed.

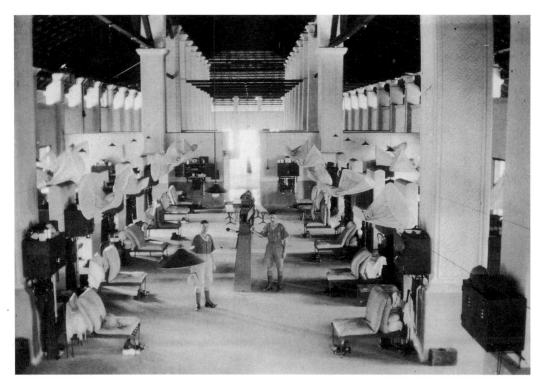

A daytime view with beds and mosquito nets folded, Tanglin Barracks, Singapore. The barrack blocks were considered to be some of the best in the Far East, being spacious and with high ceilings to allow the free flow of air. The 1st Battalion had arrived here from Malaya in 1933, and remained until 1936 when it went to India.

Nine recruits for the Wiltshire Regiment as they appeared at the Regimental Depot, Le Marchant Barracks, Devizes, c.1935. They were part of a thirty-man squad. Their training, which took six months, consisted of both physical and educational development. A great deal of effort went into recruiting Wiltshire men for the Wiltshire Regiment, but the rural nature of the county meant it was necessary to go further afield, to London and Birmingham for instance, to get sufficient numbers.

The same men after completing six months service, now ready to join the Home Service Battalion where they would be subjected to continuation training to bring them up to battalion standards. The regimental literature of the day states 'Food, this of course must be of the very best, and containing all those fascinating Vitamins we read about'. Most recruits had gained around 10lb by the time they left the depot.

The 2nd Battalion moved to barracks in Catterick, Yorkshire, in 1938 where they remained until the outbreak of the Second World War. Shown here is the 2nd Battalion motor-cycle team at the start of the Army Motor Cycle Championship, 1939. From left to right: Cpl Wright; Lt Archer; Pte Gatehouse. Points were awarded for speed, map-reading and the ability to move the motor cycle over rugged terrain. The battalion did not win the Championship but the motor cyclists' skills were tested for real the following year on the retreat to Dunkirk, where on many occasions the only means of communication was via the 'Donar' [Dispatch rider].

4th Battalion on Exercise 'Bumper', c.1940. After Dunkirk, and in the lead up to the Normandy landings in 1944, the 43rd Wessex Division, of which the 4th Battalion formed part, extensively trained in the South of England. As a consequence, their 'barracks' when on exercises were barns, ditches and anywhere else they could shelter from the weather conditions. It had the effect of hardening the battalion up for what followed in Normandy. Here we see members of the battalion carrying out their ablutions at the village pump in Winslow, Buckinghamshire, watched over by interested locals.

An inspection of the Wiltshire Army Cadet Corps of Drums, Le Marchant Barracks, Devizes, c.1944. During the Second World War, the regiment transferred its training to Colchester. The Devizes Barracks were used for cadet training, an activity which was encouraged as it enabled young men to get early experience of basic soldiering skills.

The brigade colonel's inspection at the Depot, Devizes, 3 January 1952. A new National Service recruit has his shirt tail marked with his regimental number by the Quartermaster's clerk Cpl Greenaway. Overseeing this highly intricate military operation are from left to right: Col. N.C.E. Kenrick, DSO; (late Wiltshire Regiment) Maj. Newton Dunn; Lt Bashall; Lt-Col. (QM) J. Newton, MBE, MM and L/Cpl Greenaway, the QM's clerk.

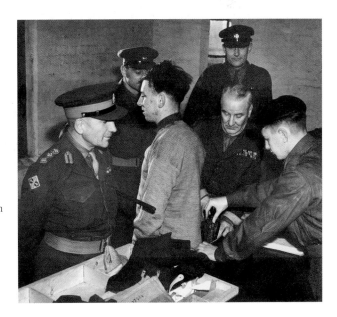

Above: The 1st Battalion arrived in Cyprus in January 1956, and spent the next three years on active service. Some members of the battalion were stationed in the twelfth-century Kyrenia Castle, seen here from the east. The castle was utilised as a base but most of the operations took place elsewhere.

Left: Inside Kyrenia Castle, Cyprus, *c.*1957. A 1st Battalion Wiltshire Regiment Lance Corporal poses for a photograph. Although a somewhat artificial image, it gives a clear impression of the conditions inside the castle at that time.

six

The Second World War

The 2nd Battalion went to France as part of the British Expeditionary Force on 14 September 1939. Here we see the Secretary of State, Stanley Oliver, inspecting a guard of honour during the 'Phoney War'. The battalion went to great lengths to maintain pre-war regimental standards. On the left is the newly appointed commander of 13 Brigade, Brig. Miles Dempsey, MC, formerly the commanding officer of the 1st Battalion Royal Berkshire Regiment, who went on to command the Second Army under General Montgomery.

In December 1939 the 2nd Battalion took up positions along the river Lys, near Armentières. In addition to normal training, the battalion provided working parties to help the Royal Engineers build 'pillboxes' along the defence line known as the 'Gort Line'. Useful experience was gained in siting defences, construction work and wiring. Shown here are 2nd Battalion soldiers at work on a pillbox in a disused chocolate factory.

Officers of the 1st Battalion, Havelock Lines, Lucknow, India 1942. From left to right, back row: 2nd/Lts Shephard, Davis, Haines, Everett; Lt Topham (wounded). Centre row: Capt. Affleck; Lt Skene; Capt. Climpson; 2nd/Lt Weatherup; Capt. Brown; Capt. Wort. Front row: Capts Magawly (accidentally shot 15.2.1944) and Stephenson; Maj. Redman; Lt-Col. Green; Capt. Day (Killed in Action 22.2.1944); Lt (QM) Newton, MM; Capt. Shadwell.

Members of the 1st Battalion receive training in the newly issued 2 inch mortar in India, c.1942. On the outbreak of war, the battalion was stationed in India. It remained there training until it joined the 26th (Tiger Head) Division in 1944. From February onwards, the battalion saw heavy fighting in the Arakan jungles of Burma.

On the outbreak of war the 4th (Territorial) Battalion mobilised and became part of 129 Brigade of the 43rd Wessex Division. It was joined in that brigade by its sister battalion, the 5th. The battalions remained together until the end of the war. Initially deployed in the Home Defence role in a number of different areas, the final destination was Kent, under General Montgomery in 12 Corps. Here we see soldiers of the 4th Battalion in full fighting order on an assault course.

The training intensified as the 4th and 5th Battalions practised all phases of war. It continued throughout the winter of 1941. In their quest for 'assault fitness' the doctrines learnt and physical exertions suffered by the officers and NCOs at the battle school at Lockailort in Scotland were immediately passed on to the soldiers of both battalions on their return. Here we see soldiers of the 4th Battalion mastering the art of scaling a rock face in full fighting order.

A rifle platoon route marching in full battle order in a Kent country lane. The 4th Battalion trained hard during this period of time with exercises 'Bumper' and 'Tiger' being remembered mostly for their physical toughness. By now the battalion were able to take part in extensive forced marches with an ever-increasing high completion rate. On one exercise, after marching almost continuously for ten days, Gen. Montgomery rewarded the men with some cases of Oxo! The training and experience of this type of terrain was to stand the battalion in good stead when fighting in the Bocage country in Normandy in 1944.

In 1942 the 2nd Battalion embarked for overseas service, destined for India. En route, the 13th Brigade (to which the 2nd Battalion belonged) took part in an assault landing at the northern end of Madagascar, which was held by the Vichy French. This took place on 5 May 1942. The brigade was in reserve, but on landing took part in a seventeen-mile night march to support the forward troops who were held up outside Antisirane. After digging in on an airfield the brigade was withdrawn and resumed the journey to India. Here we see soldiers of the 2nd Battalion with the locals. Standing at the back on the left is Sgt Maurice Rogers, who later won the Victoria Cross in Italy.

After a variety of stations in the Middle East the 2nd Battalion was back in Europe by 1943, taking part in the invasion of Sicily on 10 July at the start of the Italian campaign. Shortly after landing, the battalion attacked Solarino, then made a four-day march through Lentini and up to the Simeto River in the Catania plain. This photograph shows heavily laden infantrymen of the battalion making their way through the village of Melilli during that march.

Capt. Culverhouse, intelligence officer of the battalion, gets some valuable news of the Germans from Guiseppe Patullo of Bojano, Sicily, through the brigade interpreter, L/Cpl Hardusty. The role of the intelligence section was crucial, not only for the commanding officer but also for senior officers behind the front line. The interrogation and identification of newly captured prisoners, and the debriefing of our own patrols, was a regular task for the battalion intelligence section.

Bren Carriers of the 2nd Battalion, moving through Paterno, Sicily, 1943. On 6 August the 2nd Battalion attacked the town which lies in the Etna foothills. It was nearly empty and was taken with no casualties. The War Diary later recorded:

PATERNO has been severely damaged by our bombs and shells and there were many civilian casualties. The RAP [Regimental Aid Post] has given all possible assistance. The local inhabitants gave us a great welcome and were very grateful for any help we could give them. They report several instances of GERMAN frightfulness.

The German unit which had previously occupied Paterno was the Hermann Goering Division, which had become renowned for its fighting qualities. On securing the town the 2nd Battalion Anti-Tank detachments seen here were moved to the outskirts to meet any counter-attacks that the Germans might make. In the event, none came. The 2nd Battalion remained in Sicily until August 1943, when it embarked for Italy.

The 2nd Battalion sailed from Sicily, in August 1943, to the Messina area of Italy. It later went by sea to Palmi, and after landing, advanced up the coastal road, encountering strong rear-guard opposition. The commanding officer, Lt-Col. Palmer, was badly wounded. After this the battalion marched all night through the mountains to Vibo Valencia, receiving news of the Italian surrender on the way. It is believed that this photograph was taken at the start of this march. For its actions in Sicily and Italy, the 2nd Battalion earned for the regiment the Battle Honours: Solarino, Simeto Bridgehead, Sicily 1943, Garigliano Crossing, Minturno, Anzio, Advance to Tiber, and Italy 1943–44.

While the 2nd Battalion fought in Italy, the 4th and 5th Battalions prepared for the Normandy campaign. After landing on 23 June, they started advancing through France. Here, the intelligence section of the 4th Battalion make their way along the Caen road at Tourville to the start line for the assault on the Villers Bocage. The section is led by Sgt Keith Young, who was badly wounded on 23 July 1944.

'B' Company, 4th Battalion, seen here moving through a 'safe lane' after arriving in France. They were called the 'Mobile Company' and issued with bicycles, which proved useless in the mud. Some were 'accidentally' lost under passing friendly tanks, and in August the battalion ceased using them. From left to right, from the rear, are: Pte Bert Dredge, Pte Jim Wicks and Pte W. Cousins. All three were later Killed in Action.

Soldiers of the 4th or 5th Battalion rest in the town of Vernon on 25 August 1944, prior to the crossing of the river Seine. The 43rd Wessex Division, including these two battalions, had made a 120-mile journey in thirty-six hours to reach the concentration area. The 4th Battalion took on responsibility for the defence of Vernon while the 5th prepared for the river crossing. Within two hours of arrival, the assault crossing started.

Soldiers of the 4th Battalion manhandle the storm boats in preparation for the river Seine assault crossing by their sister battalion, the 5th. It took around thirty-six troops to move one boat, and with sixteen to be carried forward, nearly 600 men were needed. Carrying parties were hurriedly made up from anyone who could be found but, even so, it took longer to get the boats to the river than had been anticipated.

A rifle section of the 5th Battalion wait under a bridge for the order to move forward. Unknown to them, the high escarpment on the opposite shore was occupied by the enemy in the form of Battle Group Meyer. A less inviting place to force a crossing would be difficult to imagine.

A section commander from 'A' Company leads his section, under cover of a smoke screen, to the water's edge ready for embarking. Their weapons have been double-checked and bayonets fixed. The order to cross the river has been given, but with only one amphibious DUKW able to be launched, the majority of the 5th are destined to cross in assault boats. This remarkable series of images is due to two official photographers being in the area.

Three riflemen embark, followed by a Bren Gunner of 'A' Company. The steep banks made it difficult for the heavily laden infantry to climb into the boats. Engineers with long boathooks held the flat-bottomed vessels close to the shore, but they still rocked violently as each man stepped forward.

Once the soldiers were aboard, the craft were pushed off and their engines started. Here we see members of 'A' Company, the first wave who had been selected under the command of Major Milne to lead the right-hand assault. Their orders were simple: cross the river and hold the right flank against any enemy interference with the bridging site.

One boat containing half of No.8 platoon under the command of Lt Selby disappeared into the smoke. Everything seemed to be going well until, with about thirty yards to go, both boats grounded on a mud bank and came to an abrupt halt. At the same time, the smoke screen began to disperse. The German response to the attempted crossing was both immediate and savage. Machine-gun bullets raked both boats. Within minutes, twenty-four men were dead, one of whom was Lt Selby. For this action, the battalion earned the Battle Honour 'Seine 1944'.

Pte Barnes of the 4th Battalion Anti-Tank Platoon, keeping a watchful eye while his pals sleep in their Bren Carrier, 21 September 1944. Hold-ups on the single road to Arnhem were a regular feature of this operation. Taking part in operation 'Market Garden', the 4th and 5th Battalion's objective was to meet up with the Airborne Forces at Arnhem. In the event, it became a rescue mission after the heroic battle by the Parachute Regiment to take the bridge, later described as a 'Bridge Too Far'.

At Valkenswaard, seven miles inside the Dutch border, the 4th Battalion was met by local people in their Sunday-best clothes. Committed to a single road, the demolition by the Germans of the bridge at Son, north of Eindhoven, delayed still further the forward movement of the relief force. Here we see troops talking to some Dutch children. From left to right: Jack Day, Arthur Hicketts, John Mewes, Jack Pike and Sam Rowlands. It was in this signal store truck that Pte Stanley Lodge was killed in Normandy on 1 August 1944.

Due to the deteriorating situation in Arnhem, the 4th Battalion was pushed to move faster in spite of the opposition it met. An order to lead the attack on the village of Elst meant crossing the bridge at Nijmegen. The battalion paused in the town because the bridge was being shelled, giving troops the chance to rest. They later went over the bridge before the mist lifted, and for the next few days the battalion was involved in ferocious fighting in and around Elst.

The 5th Battalion take over the village of Breberen, Germany, during Operation 'Baldock', 21 January 1945. Here we see soldiers of the battalion moving into position, some wearing snow smocks, others with white painted gas capes. The battalion remained in the village, holding it against enemy counter attacks until 25 January when it moved forward to the start line to attack the village of Utterath.

The 5th Battalion occupied Calcar on 27 February 1945, and took up defensive positions. Here we see a forward Bren gun trench in March 1945. At the rear of the trench is Cpl Campbell, who was later described by a member of his section as, 'the greatest fighting Cpl and section commander to be born'. From this location, on 7 March they took part in a major attack on Luttingen. The regimental history records, 'Eventually Lt Massey received orders to withdraw his platoon. He sent his men back in small groups while he remained himself to the last with Corporal Campbell and Pte Etheridge keeping up a constant fire with the bren gun, until the men were safely clear'. The day following the battle forty-seven dead Germans were counted in those trenches. The 4th and 5th Battalions earned the Battle Honours: Odon, Caen, Hill 112, Bourguebus Ridge, Maltot, Mont Pincon, La Variniere, Seine 1944, Nederrjin, Roer, Rhineland, Cleve, Goch, Xanten, Rhine, Bremen, and North-West Europe 1944–45.

Officers of the 1st Battalion, Victoria Barracks, Rawalpindi, India, c.1945. These officers served in the Arakan. From left to right, back row: Lt Borwick; Dr Gibb; Capt. Avery (Signal Officer); Saville; Haines; Capt. Adams (Intelligence Officer); Capt. Affleck; Capt. (QM) 'Inky' Penn. Centre row: Brown; Falks; Redman; Pawes; Lt-Col. Houghton-Brown (Commanding Officer) (wounded); Capt. Townsend; Capt. Cain (Adjutant); Capt. Motion; Johner. Front row: Macklin; Horsley; Davey; Colvin; Murphy; Brooks; Mackay; Merrett.

After serving in Burma, the 1st Battalion returned to India and in March 1945 were deployed to the North West Frontier. Here we see members of a rifle section in a *sangar* [rock emplacement] at Razmak. Dominating the high ground was a lesson generations of soldiers in India very quickly learned. From left to right: L/Cpl –?–, Ptes Bill Bates, Ted McNulty, Sid Rowe, and 'Bronco' Reid. The opposition here were the Pathan tribesmen On one evening raid, Pte McNulty was injured by a bayonet, but survived to tell the tale.

Soldiers of 'C' Company, 1st Battalion, de-bus prior to an operation to 'open the road' at Razmak, *c*.1945. This was a tactic used to keep lines of communication open between garrisons on the frontier. The sergeant on the left is 'Chesty' Yates. Very few of these operations went by without some sort of sniping activity from local tribesmen. On 11 August 1945, the battalion's only fatal casualty during this tour was Pte Wakefield, who was killed by a sniper.

The county of Wiltshire raised thirteen battalions of Home Guard units during the Second World War, in addition to smaller units such as the 220th (101st Wiltshire Home Guard) Rocket A.A. Battery and 2142 (Wiltshire) Home Guard M.T. Company. Here we see members of No.4 (Devizes) Company marching through Devizes to a church parade behind their own band. One member of the Wiltshire Home Guard, Lt W. Foster, MC, DCM, was posthumously awarded the George Cross for throwing himself on a live grenade during grenade-throwing practice. His actions saved the life of a comrade.

The 2nd Battalion as the lead battalion in 13 Brigade advance on the outskirts of Lubeck, Germany, May 1945. Clearing the village of Molln after some scattered resistance the battalion had a rifle company in Ratzeberg later the same day. Continuing to move at speed, it soon reached Grosse Gronau, only five miles from Lubeck, where this picture was taken on 2 May.

On the road to Lubeck, 2 May 1945. Laden infantrymen of the 2nd Battalion advance along a hedgerow. The tanks on the road behind these soldiers relied heavily on infantry support in this type of terrain.

There was some resistance from a few fanatics armed with LMGs and light anti-tank weapons on the southern outskirts of the village. This was overcome after a short sharp fight by the vanguard. About 300 Germans, mostly old men, were found in the northern half of the village waiting to give themselves up. Battalion casualties were one officer and four ORs wounded. Here we see two stretcher bearers of the 2nd Battalion tending a wounded German during this action.

On the way to Lubeck the 2nd Battalion had to contend with surrendering German Army units plus members of the German home guard (The Volkstrum). Shown here is a lone heavily armed infantryman of the 2nd Battalion, 'ushering' back a number of Prisoners of War

Soldiers of the 2nd Battalion near Lubeck, Germany, May 1945. From left to right: Sgt Myland, Pte 'Ozzie' Osbourne, Sgt 'Spot' Taylor, Pte 'Lofty' Hillier, CSM Whitemarsh, Cpl Bone. The battalion had just fought a short action and discovered Sgt Taylor, a Wiltshire Regiment Prisoner of War. He had been captured in Italy while serving with the 2nd Battalion, and then transported to Germany. As the allies advanced, prisoners were left by the retreating Germans to fend for themselves. 'Lofty' Hillier later wrote in his book, *The Long Road to Victory*:

> We pushed on and struck another Stalag, and this time it was all British men. As we were opening the gates a voice said 'How in the hell did you get here, I left you in Italy. I always told this lot it would be you that would relieve us.' It was one of our Sgts (Sgt Taylor) who was captured at the Minturno ridge during the first battle for Cassino.

One of the group took a quick photograph then the advance continued, leaving Sgt Taylor to be taken care of by follow-up units.

Sgt Goubey of the 2nd Battalion offers a mug of tea to newly released Royal Air Force Prisoners of War who now find themselves at last on the right side of the line after the departure of their German guards, May 1945. The heavily laden infantrymen in the truck are no doubt grateful for the transport. The 'Y' formation sign on the soldier's arm is the divisional formation sign of the 5th Division, of which the 2nd Battalion were a part. The 'Y' came about because the division was formed in Yorkshire.

Ramzak, August 1945. The 1st Battalion celebrate VJ Day. The last British battalion to garrison the town, the 1st moved out to Rawalpindi in December the same year. It left the North-West Frontier with the good record of having had only one fatal casualty, of never having been ambushed and of losing no weapons to the local tribesmen. During its time in action in Burma, the battalion earned the Battle Honours North Arakan, Point 551, Mayu Tunnels, Ngakyedauk Pass, and Burma 1943–44.

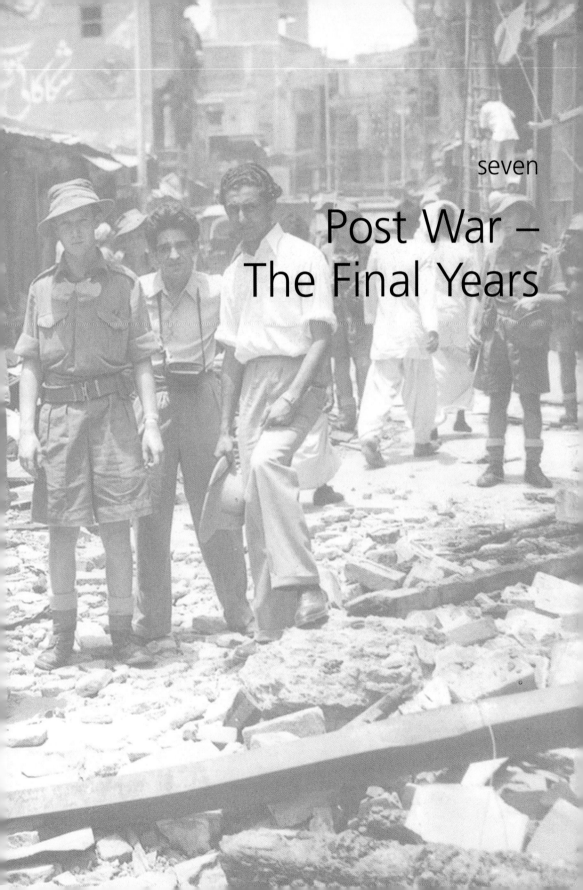

seven

Post War –
The Final Years

Durbar Hall, Lahore Fort, May 1947. After the Second World War, the 1st Battalion remained in India. It was one of the units that were deployed in preserving the peace between the various factions in the months leading up to partition. Here we see 'C' Company resting after patrolling the divided city. On the right, facing the camera with his hand on his chin, is Lt-Col. Kenrick, the commanding officer, and behind him Capt. Fine talks to two local police officers.

The 1st Battalion remained in Lahore for nine weeks, operating in temperatures that often rose to 118°F in the shade. Here, Lt-Col. Kenrick (facing the camera with his hand on his hip) escorts newspaper correspondents in Lahore City to see the damage caused by the inter-communal rioting that cost many lives. In the background, members of 'C' Company provide armed protection.

In March 1948 the 2nd Battalion moved to Krefeld, near Dusseldorf, Germany. At the time, it was the only British battalion west of the Rhine. In October, what remained of the 1st Battalion came to Krefeld, and both battalions amalgamated in January 1949 to become the new 1st Battalion. This formed part of British Army of the Rhine and took part in many exercises, but parade smartness was not forgotten. Shown here is the Regimental Colour being 'Trooped' during the 1949 Ferozeshah parade. The two officers at the salute in the foreground are, from left to right: Lt G.T.L.M. Graham; RSM Bull, in the beret; Maj. D.C. Gilson, MC.

Sgt Don Briggs, seen here standing on the platform trolley, was a regular soldier and battalion boxer. Here he supervises the loading of the kitbags prior to the march to Le Marchant Barracks, April 1950. The 1st Battalion arrived at Devizes Railway Station, having travelled from Krefeld. All the worldly goods that soldiers possessed had to be carried in these kitbags. The image clearly shows the type of equipment worn by these National Service soldiers, battle dress with the cloth title 'Wiltshire' on each shoulder, with '37 pattern equipment with the 303 Lee Enfield No.4 Rifle.

Devizes, Wiltshire, April 1950. The band and drums lead Headquarters Company, 1st Battalion, through the town from the railway station to the Regimental Depot, Le Marchant Barracks. This was the first time a regular battalion had been based in the Regimental Depot. On arrival, the soldiers were divided into two groups: the 'Malaya Party' who were destined for future operations in Malaya, and the 'Details' who were eligible for demob.

On 1 August 1950, the main body of the 1st Battalion marched through Devizes to the railway station en route to Southampton, where they embarked for Malaya. Here the battalion passes the pond at Devizes, one of several in Wiltshire claiming to be the original of the 'Moonrakers' legend. To the right is Southbroom church, which holds many regimental memorials and Colours.

The 1st Battalion advance party in Malaya, 1950, practicing patrol skills in the jungle in preparation for the arrival of the rest of the battalion. They were due to relieve the 1st Devons, and the first reconnaissances were carried out by the commanding officer. After initial training, they operated with the 1st Battalion Suffolk Regiment to gain experience. In August the news came through that the main body of the battalion had been diverted to Hong Kong, so they handed in their kit and redeployed to Hong Kong. Members of this party were awarded the General Service Medal (Malaya). From left to right: Cpl Crockett, Pte Arnold and Cpl Hughes.

The arrival of the 1st Battalion at Hong Kong, 5 September 1950. During the journey on the Troopship *Empire Trooper* the battalion had learned of the change in destination when a BBC broadcast announced it on a news bulletin, telling the troops that they were now heading for Hong Kong to replace troops who had been sent to Korea. On arrival, the band of the King's Own Scottish Borderers played them in. They then made their way to Tan Mi Camp in the New Territories. Because of the Korean War, the battalion had to be ready for any eventuality on the border. As a result, there was a continuous stream of tactical exercises in addition to defence construction.

Above: On 16 March 1951 a party of 100 men, under the command of Lt A.E. Carter, left Hong Kong to join the 1st Battalion Gloucestershire Regiment in Korea. Most of these soldiers were volunteers, comprising 75 per cent National Servicemen. The men were divided into three parties. One group went to the 1st Battalion Gloucestershire Regiment two days before the Battle of the Imjin. As a result, some forty members of this draft were posted as 'Missing'. Here we see members of 'B' Company leaving Hong Kong: L/Cpl Pike, Pte Burder, Pte Shurmer, L/Cpl Reynolds.

Left: An unidentified soldier of the Wiltshire Regiment standing guard while a Chinese Prisoner of War has a wound on his head dressed. The rest of the prisoners sit at the roadside. The remaining two groups joined the re-formed Glosters after the Imjin battle, and remained with them for the rest of the tour. Sgt Eames, who had been the Sergeants' Mess caterer in Krefeld, was already serving with the Glosters. He won the Military Medal at the Battle of Hill 327, but was Killed in Action at the Imjin.

On 23 November 1951, the 1st Battalion Gloucestershire Regiment returned to England via Hong Kong, bringing with it what remained of the Wiltshire Regiment contingent. They arrived and were met at Kowloon Docks by the battalion band, who marched them to the 40th Infantry Division leave centre where they were entertained by the battalion. Many of those left behind in Korea were to spend several years in dreadful conditions in Chinese PoW camps. One ex-Corps of Drums member, 'Lofty' Large, went on to serve in the Special Air Service after being released, and wrote an account of his experiences in captivity. Here we see returned soldiers having a drink with old comrades. From left to right: -?-, Sgt Smith (Wilts Regt), Cpl Clarke (Glosters), Sgt Slark (Wilts Regt). Little did these soldiers know that years later in 1994, both regiments would be serving under the same regimental title, The Royal Gloucestershire, Berkshire and Wiltshire Regiment.

The 1st Battalion were stationed in the New Territories on the Chinese mainland some thirty miles from Hong Kong. It was decided to build a barbed-wire obstacle across the New Territories, up to 300 yards deep, with defensive positions behind that known as screening positions. However, the local authority would not allow the two roads in the area to be closed and the Royal Hong Kong Golf Course to remain untouched. The official interference prolonged the length of time needed to complete the defence works, despite the Chinese Army being on Hong Kong's doorstep. Here we see the Command Post position.

Above: The 1st Battalion's Royal Irish Cup team, 1952. Shooting competitions were taken very seriously, with the commanding officer ensuring full participation. From left to right, back row: Sgt P. Nichols; Sgt P. Martin; Sgt J. Dunkin. Front row: CQMS D. Mortimer; RSM S. Kirkbright; Lt-Col. L. Wood, OBE (Commanding Officer); Sgt W. Clare (REME); CQMS F. Chamberline. CQMS Mortimer remained with the Wiltshires and joined the Duke of Edinburgh's Royal Regiment on amalgamation in 1959. He then became the second Regimental sergeant-major of the new battalion in 1963. Sgt P. Martin retained his shooting interests, both in the military and civilian fields, with outstanding results, long after most would have hung up their rifles.

After returning from Hong Kong, the 1st Battalion became the demonstration battalion at the School of Infantry, Warminster, Wiltshire. It was here that the latest weapons and tactics were tried out. In November 1954, the Colonel-in-Chief, HRH The Duke of Edinburgh, visited the battalion. Here a rifle section demonstrates the use of the 'monkey bar' obstacle on the assault course.

Right: The Duke of Edinburgh speaks to a lance corporal section commander who stands with his section in front of a freshly dug slit trench during one of the demonstrations. These soldiers are wearing battle dress with pattern '37 webbing equipment. The battle dress had been worn by the British Army since 1940, and was not waterproof in any way. The combat suit, introduced around 1959/60, made a significant improvement to the wellbeing of troops in the field.

Opposite below: While the battalion's best shots took part in competitions, other soldiers had to reach a certain standard each year. Here we see members of the 1st Battalion on the Kai Tak ranges, preparing to carry out a Bren Gun shoot during an Army competition, *c.*1952. Nearest the camera is Sgt Stan Dunn, a regular soldier who served in the Wiltshire Regiment, Gloucestershire Regiment and the Duke of Edinburgh's Royal Regiment.

The 1st Battalion were based at Knook Camp, Warminster. Here, the Colonel-in-Chief pays close attention to the guard. He is escorted by Capt. Fladgate. On the left (carrying the Colour) is Lt Oldfield. This was the first time the new F.N. rifle had been used on an official occasion; the 303 No.4 Lee Enfield rifle had yet to be superseded within the Army and the F.N. was introduced merely as an urgent stop gap before a modified version appeared as the SLR.

The end of the Ferozeshah Parade, Warminster, December 1955. The parade was attended by the Colonel-in-Chief, HRH The Duke of Edinburgh. The sergeants have taken over the Colours from the officers, and will retain them until midnight. Here we see the drum major preparing the Colours for re-casing. The escort present arms. From left to right: Drum Major Pegg (whose son served in the amalgamated regiment The Duke of Edinburgh's Royal Regiment); CQMS Brown; CSM Young and CQMS Normington.

In 1957 it was decided that one territorial unit per command would be sent each year to Millom, in Cumberland, to undergo a limited course in Civil Defence training during their Annual Camp. The 4th Battalion were the first unit to attend, and here we see soldiers from 'D' Company practicing the removal of injured persons from destroyed buildings. From left to right: Cpl Flippance and Pte Stone, both from Swindon.

The 4th Battalion spent most of their two weeks of Civil Defence training on this type of exercise. The journal records, 'The course was quite strenuous and the thirsts that ensued helped the evenings in the Mess to go with a swing or should we say "swig"'. The 1950s and 1960s saw the Cold War reach its height, and nominated TA battalions had Civil Defence training high on their priorities. The Army and Police earmarked 'flying columns', designed to operate as independent units anywhere in the country in the event of nuclear attack.

The 1st Battalion arrived in Cyprus in January 1956, and remained on Active Service for the following three years. Here we see riot control and crowd dispersal training inside Kyrenia Castle, c.1957. This constant close contact training was essential for those involved to understand how any live situation might develop and the best way of dealing with it. The officer controlling this particular exercise is 2nd/Lt Holroyd, who can just be seen in the centre. He was a National Service Officer serving with the battalion during 1956–57. He completed his National Service commitment with the 4th Battalion, after attending Oxford University. He later became an Under Secretary of State in the Ministry of Agriculture.

This type of training continued throughout the 1st Battalion's tour in Cyprus. In spite of the inevitable accidental injuries, the training paid dividends during live operations. Such an incident was reported in the *Sunday Pictorial* on 11 March 1956: 'Seething with anger at the deportation of Archbishop Makarios, Cypriots clashed with British troops in a series of ugly incidents yesterday. Men of the Wiltshire Regiment were heavily stoned. They fought back with tear gas and made some arrests'.

Duke of Edinburgh Trophy team 1957, Cyprus. This competition was instituted by the Duke of Edinburgh for all those units of which he was the Capt. General, Colonel-in-Chief, Hon. Col. or Hon. Air Commodore. It consisted of marksmanship and endurance conducted over a thirty-six-hour period. The previous year the battalion had won the trophy, but in 1957 a change in the rules increased the team size from eight to twelve. This caused problems for the battalion who were heavily committed on operations against the EOKA terrorists. Here we see members of the team completing the 200-yard carry on the road to the rifle range, where their marksmanship skills were tested to the limit.

The team was led by Capt. G.T.L.M. Graham. He was an excellent shot who had obtained a score of 154 out of a possible of 160 the previous year, the highest in the competition. Fifteen units competed in 1957, with the 1st Battalion coming third in the trophy, despite the heavy operational commitments. From left to right, third row: Capt. DIM Robbins, MC; -?-; -?-; Cpl Pavey. Second row, sitting: Capt. Graham; Lt-Col. Hunter (Commanding Officer). As a retired Colonel, Capt. G.T.L.M. Graham later became Secretary of the Army Rifle Association.

The 4th Battalion competed in the Territorial Army's equivalent competition, winning the trophy in 1958 and 1959. In 1966 the 4th Battalion won the main competition, a considerable achievement for a non-regular unit. Shown here are members of the team conducting 'the carry', prior to the shooting section. The soldier being carried at the front is Pte David Fielding. He later joined the Duke of Edinburgh's Royal Regiment, retiring as a warrant officer.

For operations in Cyprus, volunteers from the battalion were sought to work as handlers for guard and tracker dogs. On 10 May 1956, the Regimental medical officer was wounded by a bomb thrown near the families' clinic in Kyrenia. 'C' Company cordoned off the area and tracker dogs such as the one shown above were used in the hunt for the bombers.

On 17 March 1956, two bombs exploded in the back of the truck shown above, used by
'B' Company 1st Battalion in Lapithos, Cyprus. Three soldiers (Cpl Clements and Ptes Gould and
Cook) received serious wounds, and Ptes Trenge and Wylde were slightly wounded. Pte Gould
died of his wounds the following day. The truck still shows some of the blast damage to the rear
wheel arch. As a result, a curfew was imposed in Lapithos, and searches commenced.

4 Platoon, 'B' Company 1st Battalion, about to set out on an operation to search the Sinai
Monastery at Vasilia during operation 'Lost Ashes'. All the rifle platoons were constantly on the
move conducting operations, ambushes, patrols and road blocks. These activities were designed to
restrict the movement of the EOKA terrorists.

Members of the machine-gun platoon take a rest while on patrol in the Buffavento Forest area under the command of Lt Cobbold, a National Service Officer. They are wearing the supposedly 'wind-proof' smocks which in fact did little to keep out the freezing wind. This platoon spent a considerable amount of time in the mountains developing a high state of physical fitness, but it did little for their primary role as machine gunners.

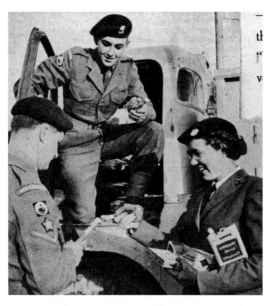

Pte Grey of the 1st Battalion looks down on Molly Johnson of the Church of Scotland, as she sells items to a Wiltshire Regiment Lance Corporal, *c.*1958. She was a welcome sight to soldiers, particularly those scattered throughout the area on company and platoon detachments, wishing to purchase a few luxuries. These civilian volunteers faced the same dangers as the troops when moving around as was demonstrated on 28 September 1956, when two vehicles of the battalion were ambushed on the outskirts of Kyrenia. The battalion's WVS helper, Mrs Holton, and Pte Read of 'A' Company were killed, and Pte Flower was wounded. As a result of this ambush, 'Operation Sparrowhawk' was mounted and the EOKA group that carried out the ambush were captured and later sentenced to life imprisonment.

Opposite above: On 22 October 1958 the officer in command of 'A' Company, 1st Battalion, was ambushed by three terrorists who prematurely set off an electrically detonated mine. Luckily there were no injuries, but despite the soldiers returning fire, the terrorists made good their escape. This set in motion a series of events that led the battalion to the Orange Grove at Karavas. Here we see members of 'A' Company carrying out a dig at a suspected arms hide using mine detectors, wire prodders, bayonets and shovels.

Above: The search was successful. The cache included three machine carbines, four pistols, three tree mortars, a double-barrelled shotgun and a mixed variety of ammunition. Among later finds were pipe bombs, a large quantity of potassium chloride and other explosives, together with typewriters and duplicators. The finds reduced EOKA activity in the area – for a while.

Operation 'Wardsworth', which took place below Kourtella in the hills of Cyprus. On the left is the commanding officer, Lt-Col. G. Woolnough, MC, and to his rear, Majors Turner and Worth. Just visible behind Lt-Col. Woolnough is the battalion signal officer, Lt Canning, whose father had also served in the regiment. In August 1969, Lt Canning's Cyprus experience proved invaluable when he took 'C' Company, 1st Battalion Duke of Edinburgh's Royal Regiment, onto the streets of Londonderry at the start of the Ulster troubles.

Company Sgt-Maj. Doug Mortimer leads the headquarters signallers of 'B' Company, 1st Battalion, on Operation 'Wardsworth'. Good communication was crucial in operations of this type, with the radio operators having to carry a considerable load. During this period of time, it was recorded that the physical fitness of the battalion was at the highest level.

Above left: Christoforou Kyriakos Matsis had been the primary target for the 1st Battalion for two years. He was detained in 1956, but escaped, then went on to organise a very efficient EOKA group in the Kyrenia district. Among the indigenous population, his name was held in awe, while every soldier knew his face from the many photographs displayed.

On 24 November 1958, as a result of information received, troops of the Wiltshire, Royal Berkshire and Parachute Regiments surrounded the small village of Kato Dhikomo and commenced a search. A soldier of the Wiltshire Regiment uncovered a hide after finding several loose tiles in a house. Matsis had been discovered at last, together with two other men. They were called upon to surrender, which the other two, both wanted men, did. Matsis refused and shouted he would come out shooting.

Above right: 'D' Company, 1st Battalion were responsible for dealing with Matsis. Seen here are the 'D' Company snatch party are, from left to right: L/Cpl Williams; L/Cpl Grey; Maj. Knott; CSM Barrow; Sgt Mills; Lt Draper and Pte Dicker. A smoke grenade was thrown in, which not only filled the hide, but the room above as well. This was followed by two Mills 36 grenades, which ended Matsis' life. Lt-Col. Woolnough, the commanding officer, when interviewed by the *Cyprus Times*, said 'We have been very successful in this operation; the object was to smash EOKA in Kyrenia and to get the leader Matsis. Even if operations stopped now EOKA would be paralysed for a long time'.

Although the operations in Cyprus provided good experience for young NCOs and officers, the posting offered little chance to practice battalion standard operations of all kinds. The maintenance of a high level of professional competence at platoon level, however, was all-important, and competitions were organised to achieve this aim. These mainly tested fitness, endurance and marksmanship. The inspecting officer would deduct points for missing or unserviceable equipment. Here, one of the rifle platoons of the 1st Battalion is inspected before such a competition.

Kyrenia Castle, *c.*1958. The officers of the 1st Battalion salute before falling out following a briefing from the commanding officer, Lt-Col. Woolnough, about the forthcoming amalgamation with the 1st Royal Berkshire Regiment. Liaison between the two battalions was facilitated by the fact that the Royal Berkshires were also in Cyprus engaged against EOKA.

The Regimental Funeral of 2nd/Lt Anthony Stephens, 1st Battalion. He was a National Service Officer who had only been with the battalion for three months before his death while rock climbing at Yaila on 17 November 1957. He was buried in Nicosia Military Cemetery, Cyprus. The soldiers on either side have their rifles in the reversed arms position. This tradition went back many years and it was recorded in 1586 at the funeral of Sir Phillip Sidney that the troops who accompanied the cortege, 'trailed their swords and muskets in the dust, and later in London 300 citizens trained for war, all held their weapons reversed.'

On 22 February 1958 a commemoration service was held at St Andrew's church, Kyrenia, for those members of the battalion who had died during the Cyprus tour of duty: 2nd/Lt A.K. Stephens; Ptes K.J. Reynolds, R. Gould, C.V. Read, A.F.J. Godsell. A plaque was unveiled and wreaths were laid on their graves by members of the Sergeants' Mess. Here we see the RSM, WO1 Jack Price with, on his left, CSM Joe Clough, and to his right, CSM Ray Marsh and Sgt Eric Skinner.

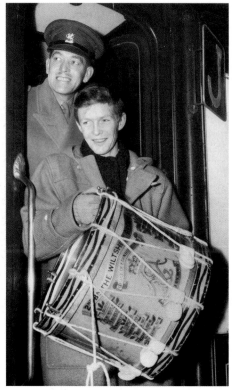

Above: The 4th Battalion took great pride in having an excellent Corps of Drums, and much time was freely given to reach and maintain a professional standard. Here we see the fifes and drums of the battalion on a practice night in Devizes. The highlight was the Regimental bicentenary celebrations which took place in Wiltshire in 1956, when the 4th Battalion represented the regiment due to the absence of the 1st Battalion on active service in Cyprus.

Above right: The return of the 2nd Battalion's drums. The battalion had managed to retain its drums throughout the bitter fighting in May 1940, even during the rearguard actions on the beach at Dunkirk. However, it had to leave them behind when it was evacuated. After the war many efforts were made to locate them, but to no avail. Nineteen years later, one of the drums was discovered in Silkeborg, Denmark, and a second in a café in Malo-les-Bains, France. Both were ceremoniously handed back to the Regiment at Le Marchant Barracks, Devizes, on 7 January 1959. Shown here is Mr R. Iversen from Denmark, with one of the drums.

Opposite above: Little Canada Holiday Village, Wootton, Isle of Wight, 1959. Operational commitments had prevented the normal Ferozeshah celebrations while the 1st Battalion was in Cyprus. It was therefore decided to hold a final parade on 24 April before amalgamation. Shown here is the return of the Colours from the sergeants to the officers at midnight. C/Sgt Briggs hands over the Regimental Colour to Drum Maj. Ford, who will in turn hand it to one of the officers. Other members of the Colour party were: RSM Price; C/Sgt Houghton; Sgt Gibbs and Sgt Kine. The following year the commemoration was carried out in the Sergeants' Mess of the 1st Battalion, Duke of Edinburgh's Royal Regiment for the first time.

Opposite below: Although the 4th Battalion maintained the Wiltshire Regiment's title until 1967, in effect this parade by the 1st Battalion on the 2 May 1959, at Albany Barracks on the Isle of Wight, was the last of the Wiltshire Regiment prior to its amalgamation with the 1st Battalion, The Royal Berkshire Regiment, the following month to form The Duke of Edinburgh's Royal Regiment (Berkshire and Wiltshire). It was to the new regiment that the traditions, heritage and good name of the Wiltshire Regiment, gathered over the previous two centuries, were now entrusted. The Colonel of the Regiment, Maj.Gen. B.A. Coad, CB, CBE, DSO takes the salute as the Colours of the 1st and 2nd Battalion are marched past.

Other titles published by Tempus

Royal Berkshire Regiment 1914–1959

MARTIN McINTYRE

The museum of the Royal Gloucestershire, Berkshire and Wiltshire Regiment contains many thousands of photographs graphically illustrating the history of the regiments. This book traces the history of the Royal Berkshire Regiment through both world wars and up to the date of its amalgamation with the Wiltshire Regiment to form the Duke of Edinburgh's Royal Regiment.

0 7524 3471 3

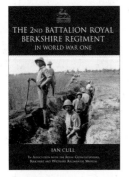

The 2nd Battalion Royal Berkshire Regiment in World War One

IAN CULL

The 2nd Royal Berkshire Regiment were a fighting force of hardened professionals recalled from guarding the Empire to face the German onslaught in August 1914. Despite countless setbacks, the Battalion never lost its spirit, and never forgot its traditions. This book covers the years between 1911 and 1919, and features many rare archive images, a richly researched history, and informative maps.

0 7524 3571 X

In Wiltshire's Skies

COLIN CRUDDAS

In 1911, Larkhill, near Durrington Down on Salisbury Plain, became Britain's first military airfield. Along with similar bases constructed at nearby Upavon and Netheravon, it was to occupy a cornerstone position in Wiltshire's early aviation history. *In Wiltshire's Skies* throws a wide net over the locations, events and many colourful personalities which have shaped the county's aeronautical heritage.

0 7524 3235 4

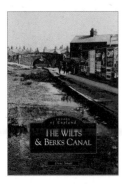

The Wilts & Berks Canal

DOUG SMALL

The Wilts & Berks was conceived in the late canal boom and, like most of those later canals, was doomed to failure. It didn't offer a shorter route to London, passed through no major town, and its main source of income, the Somerset coalfield, was soon worked out. The canal was abandoned as towns like Abingdon, Swindon and Chippenham grew around it. This book traces its past.

0 7524 1619 7

If you are interested in purchasing other books published by Tempus, or in case you have difficulty finding any Tempus books in your local bookshop, you can also place orders directly through our website

www.tempus-publishing.com